W9-BPM-980

Red Sky *in* Mourning

The true story of a woman's courage and survival at sea.

WRITTEN BY
TAMI OLDHAM ASHCRAFT

With
Susea McGearhart

Copyright © 1998 by Tami Oldham Ashcraft
All rights reserved.
This book or parts thereof, may not be reproduced in any form
without permission. For information about permission, write to

Bright Works Publishing

Published by:
Bright Works Publishing
P.O. Box 2154, Friday Harbor, WA 98250

Phone/Fax: (360) 378-6776
email: ashcraft@rockisland.com
website: www.rockisland.com/~ashcraft

Library of Congress Catalog Card Number: 96-09538

ISBN 0-9655837-7-5

Printed in the United States
1 2 3 4 5 6 7 8 9 10
Book design, layout, cover, and maps by Bruce Conway
Friday Harbor, Washington

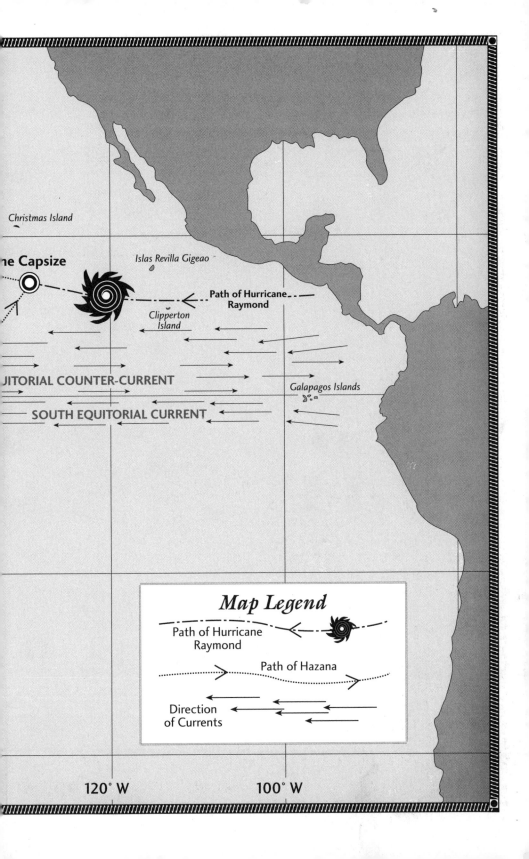

Christmas Island

ne Capsize

Islas Revilla Gigeao

Clipperton
Island

Path of Hurricane
Raymond

EQUITORIAL COUNTER-CURRENT

Galapagos Islands

SOUTH EQUITORIAL CURRENT

Map Legend

Path of Hurricane
Raymond

Path of Hazana

Direction
of Currents

120° W   100° W

Red Sky
in
Mourning

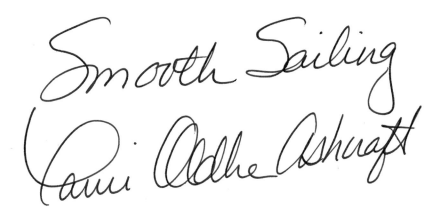

Smooth Sailing

Tami Oldham Ashcraft

Dedicated to the memory of my grandfather
Wally J. Oldham.
The solid foundation in my life.

RED SKY IN MOURNING

Table of Contents

RED SKY IN MOURNING

Acknowledgments

Without the help and dedication of many people the thought of putting my story into a book would have been left at that—a thought. Through all the twists and turns, this book has taken a life of its own. I would like to thank the many people who have helped it unfold and to my friends and family for your never ending support.

I am especially grateful to Marie Ashcraft for earnestly editing every revision. To Oscar Lind, who's been a beacon in the fog. Lynne Mercer for her "walk your talk" challenge. Debbie Bledsoe whose energy is contagious. Mitzi Johnson for her conceptualization. Steve and Eric Brandt for giving me invaluable guidance and inspiration. Teri Thompson Hodges, Cathy Johnson, Mary Stone, Neva Beach, Amanda Swan and Gerard Woldtvedt for the hours of editing that kept this project on track, and to Bruce Conway who is truly a magician with a Macintosh and whose advice was spot-on.

I am truly indebted to Susea McGearhart for her enthusiasm and focus on this project, without whom this book would still be just a dream.

And thank you Gene Gearhart for casting Susea off on this long writing voyage.

Thank you to my family.

To my mother for giving me drive and the strength to tackle life head on.

My grandma and grandpa Oldham for instilling their values and being the stability in my life.

My father and step-mother for their moral support and living proof of how to have fun in life.

My little brother Dane (who is not so little) for giving me the will to live when I was at my lowest.

To the love of my life, Ed, thank you for your total commitment to me and our family. Your patience through this project was staggering.

Thanks to my girls Kelli and Brook who have taught me about unconditional love and unbeknownst to me then but the real reason I lived.

Chapter One

On The Firing Line

Hearing the clank of the anchor shank as it hit the bow roller, I turned my attention to Richard. With a grand gesture, he waved come on—"Let's go!" I shifted the engine to forward. As I nudged the throttle, *Hazana* gathered speed and we headed out of Papeete Harbor on the island of Tahiti. It was September 22, 1983, at 1330. In a month we'd be back in San Diego, California. If only I were more excited. I hated to leave the South Pacific. It wasn't that I didn't want to see my family and friends, it was just too soon. We'd only been gone six months from California and had originally planned to cruise the South Pacific islands and New Zealand before visiting home again. This interruption to our plan left me feeling pensive. But as Richard pointed out, this yacht delivery job was a dream come true—too good to pass up.

Shouts from the shore drew my attention. Turning around, I saw some of our friends waving good-bye. I stood up on the helm seat and waved with both arms high in the air as I steered with my bare left foot. I felt a pinch on my big toe as Richard took the helm with one arm and put the other around my waist. I looked down into his China-blue eyes. They were full of joy. He squeezed me close and kissed my pareu covered stomach. I couldn't help but smile, he was like a young boy in his excitement.

"Anchors aweigh, love."

"Yep, anchors aweigh!" I chimed back.

My eyes teared as I gave one final wave to the friends on the wharf who now appeared as lampposts on the quay. The familiar knot in my throat was a reminder of how hard it always is to leave, the thought that you may never meet again. Even though we will be back soon, I reminded myself, our friends will probably not be there. Sailors don't stay long in one place—they travel on.

I took the wheel as Richard went to hoist the mainsail. Taking a deep breath I scanned the horizon. The island of Moorea stood out to the northwest. Oh, how I loved the sea! Steering the boat into the wind, the mainsail cracked and flogged as Richard launched the canvas up the sail track. Turning the boat downwind, the roller-furling jib escaped as slickly as a raindrop on glass. *Hazana* comfortably heeled over. What a yacht this Trintella is, I thought. Forty-four feet of precision. So plush compared to our *Mayaluga*.

Watching Richard trim *Hazana's* sails, I reflected on how hard it had been for him to say good-bye to *Mayaluga*. He had built her in South Africa and he named her after the Swazi word, "One who goes over the horizon." She had been his home for many years, and he had sailed the thirty-six-foot, Ferro cement cutter, half way around the world. *Mayaluga's* lines were sleek and pleasing to the eye, her interior a craftsman's dream, with laminated mahogany deck beams gleaming from layers of velvety varnish and a teak and holly sole. Poor *Mayaluga*, left alone at anchor in the bay at Mataiea.

Yacht Mayaluga

To avoid thinking too much about what we would be leaving behind, we both kept busy. I was preoccupied in trying to assemble all the clothes and personal things we would need in the

Richard and I aboard Mayaluga

two hemispheres we'd be sailing through and visiting in the next four months: T-shirts for fall in San Diego. Jackets for Christmas in England. Sweatshirts for early winter back in San Diego. Pareus and shorts for our return in late January to Tahiti. Richard had focused on preparing *Mayaluga* for the months ahead without us.

She'd be safe in Mataiea Bay. We took special care to close all the valves, except the one to the engine. Our friend Haipade, who lives at the bay with his wife Antoinette and their three children, promised to run her engine for us once a week. We took special care to prop up all the cushions and boards so the humid air of Tahiti could circulate. We left the big awning up to help protect her brightwork from the intense sun and cracked a hatch under the awning.

When we left *Mayaluga* my back was turned to her as Richard rowed us to shore. I could not see his eyes through his sunglasses, but I knew they were misty. "I know Haipade will take good care of her." I confided.

"Yeah, he will. This bay is completely protected."

"Besides, we'll be back in no time. Right?"

"Right—oh." Knowingly he smiled at me for I had mimicked his British accent.

As the wind shifted, I altered *Hazana*'s course ten degrees. Richard leaned down in front of me blocking my view. "You okay?"

"Sure."

Going behind me he uncleated the halyard to raise the mizzen sail. "Isn't this great?"

It was great. Perfect weather, perfect wind, and perfect company. His optimism was contagious. Isn't this what sailing's all about, I thought? Adventure. Going for it. Hell—time would fly.

The log entry for our first day out read: "Perfect day. Tetiaroa abeam. Full moon. Making 5 kts. in calm sea under all plain sail."

Yacht Hazana, a Trintella 44'

Day Two, we were making six knots under the mainsail and double headsails. Later in the day we had to sheet all the sails in hard to combat the north-northeast wind.

Day Three we were still pounding into the wind. *Hazana* held up well, but we felt fatigued. A thirty-five knot squall hit later in the day. We rolled in the genny, dropped the mainsail, and sailed under staysail and mizzen.

The clap of a wave

against *Hazana*'s port bow startled me. I ducked my head to keep from getting spray in my face. There was no way we'd be easing the sheets for awhile. We had committed to delivering *Hazana*, and it was San Diego or bust.

When I first started sailing I never looked back. I just went for it. Thank God Richard is nothing like Fred—good old Fred.

The sign Fred posted on the bulletin board at the small outdoor restaurant in Cabo San Lucas read: "Crew wanted. Sailing experience not necessary. Cooking a must. Departing for French Polynesia at the end of the month." I didn't even know where French Polynesia was, but I was ready for adventure, so I met with him and we discussed what my responsibilities as a crewmate would be on board *Tangaroa*, his Dreadnought 32. I told Fred the only boat I'd ever sailed was my dad's Hobie Cat in San Diego Bay, so I didn't know a thing about sailing, let alone sailing across the ocean to foreign ports. And if what he really wanted was a "partner," I wasn't interested. He told me he was recovering from a Tabasco-laden divorce and the last thing in the world he wanted or needed was a "partner." All I would need to do was cook and stand watch.

Fred and I were like oil and water. He, mid-fifties, liked classical music. I almost twenty, liked rock 'n roll. He liked gourmet cuisine. I liked vegetarian meals. Fred was very disciplined. I was very carefree. He was an impressive man in that his posture was perfect, his body perfect, and his tan perfect. But all that was way too perfect for me. I could hardly wait to get off *Tangaroa* after the thirty-one-day passage to the Marquesas. By the time we arrived, Fred and I were barely speaking.

Unfortunately the money I carried was in pesos, which the Marquesans don't recognize as a trading currency. Fred posted the $850 bond for me, but it meant I had to keep crewing and cooking for him. I mailed my pesos to my mom, in San Diego, California, who promised to convert them to American dollars and mail the exchange back to me.

About that time I met a young woman named Darla, who was also crewing on a yacht, and we became fast friends. A small group of us crewmates, all about the same age, ended up fraternizing, and to keep us from committing mutiny, our captains decided to buddy-boat together through the Marquesas Island group.

Fred and I were the first boat in our group to leave the Marquesas and head for the Tuamotu Archipelago. It would be a three-day trip, and we deliberately timed it to arrive on a full moon, which would give us the most available light at night in case we arrived later than planned.

Because atolls are not easily seen they are very dangerous to the mariner. The highest point on an atoll is the palm tree, and the land on which the palm tree grows is only visible within a couple of miles.

Fred and I had been told to look for certain ships and boats that had gone aground on the atolls, and to use these old hulks as points of navigation. Sailing past some of the wrecks on the reefs made me realize how important it is that everyone on board a boat be aware of the dangers and know how to navigate through hazardous areas. Something I thought Fred knew.

Our first port of call was to be Manihi. Fred calculated it would be early morning before we spotted the atoll, giving us plenty of time and good light to see the lagoon entrance and make our way in safely. When late morning came and we still hadn't seen anything, I was starting to get worried. Just about noon, we saw palms blowing in the distance. It took us over two hours to get close enough to try to locate the entrance shown on the chart. We sailed completely around the atoll, but didn't find an entrance. I was really nervous now. Even though Fred didn't want to admit it, we were lost and the sun was setting.

We decided we must have been set—that is, pushed—to the west, and that we had circumnavigated the atoll Ahe instead of Manihi. So we agreed to sail on through the night to Rangiroa.

Both of us were on edge that night. We stayed awake, watching and listening for any waves that might be breaking across a reef. It was that night, in my fear, I realized I never wanted to be in such a position again. That I needed to learn to navigate.

At first light we saw our destination. Around mid-morning, we located the pass and started through the entrance. We could see a yacht, flying an American flag, tied to the village loading dock. There was just enough room for two yachts to tie up. We maneuvered in with help from the couple off the other boat. I jumped on the dock and exhaustedly said to the woman: "Man, am I glad to be here in Rangiroa."

"Rangiroa? You're not in Rangiroa. You're in Apataki!"

I was shocked. I climbed back on board *Tangaroa* and went below to look at the chart. We had been set over a hundred miles southeast. What we thought was the atoll of Manihi, had actually been the atoll Takaroa.

I got off of *Tangaroa*, having lost confidence in Fred, and walked over to the Americans and begged them to let me crew on their boat to Tahiti. But there was no way I could change boats because my papers and bond could not be switched to another boat on the remote atoll of Apataki.

Fred and I spent a couple of days in Apataki doing minor repairs and recouping before we sailed for Tahiti. I couldn't appreciate the beauty of the small atoll because of my anger toward him. I did my best to stay out of Fred's way knowing it wouldn't be long before I would be off the boat and he would be out of my life forever. The passage took five days. But three days prior to arrival, I was all packed, ready to jump ship.

As I hopped off Fred's boat I heard, "Hey, Tami, what took you so long?" Running across the hot street in Tahiti was my friend Darla. Her blond braids flying, her multicolored pareu a streaming rainbow that hugged her thin, tanned body. I remembered how happy I was to see her. We

The Schooner Sofia

hugged and laughed. She told me her rich boyfriend was flying in the next day, and that she had reserved a bungalow for them at one of the quaint Papeete hotels.

"Come on. There's room for all of us." The offering was music to my ears as I hadn't taken a real shower or slept in a real bed for months. With a new spring in my step, off we went, arms flailing, mouths going.

When our friend Joey came to the hotel to use the shower, he told us he had signed on the schooner *Sofia* as a cook. I asked about *Sofia*. She wasn't a luxury liner by any means, he said, having been built in 1921, but she was awesome: a 123-foot, three-masted topsail schooner and cooperatively owned. He added that the accommodations were rugged: The head, for example, was a toilet seat mounted on a metal bowl located on the aft deck, rigged to dump overboard. The galley had four kerosene burners, one large diesel stove, and the sink pumped only saltwater. Fresh water was allowed for drinking and cooking only, not to be wasted on such frivolous things as rinsing saltwater off of the dishes.

People who wanted to join the cooperative paid three thousand dollars as a membership fee and got their own bunk. The cooks only had to pay fifteen hundred dollars for a membership fee. Joey set the hook when he told me the crew of *Sofia* was looking for someone to fill the other part-time cook's position. The next day I went to the schooner, applied and got the position, becoming a permanent crew member.

Though primitive, *Sofia* did have character. She carried a crew of ten to sixteen people. Her ribs creaked of history and adventure. She was heading for New Zealand via all the South Pacific island groups. Those days on *Sofia* were some of the best imaginable. The freedom of being on crystal blue water while sailing a square-rigger in glorious sunshine was magic. The camaraderie of the crew was well balanced. I was able to learn my sailing and bosun skills and the basics of navigation, as well as cooking and how to help organize and instruct people on the art of sailing. It was like being in college: *Sofia*— "U.–S.–Sea."

Once in New Zealand we headed for a little town called Nelson, located on the northern tip of the South Island in Cook Strait. We stayed for a year and a half to do some work on *Sofia*. Many crew members left, but those who stayed took odd jobs to earn more money so they could continue cruising.

I was offered a fishing job on a boat named the *Pandora*. She was owned and operated by a former *Sofia* crew member who stopped by the ship looking for crew. I signed on for an albacore season and ended up fishing two albacore seasons and a grouper season. The money was good, and I loved the challenging life of fishing. Plus, I was able to see a lot of New Zealand by water.

While I was fishing, *Sofia* received a movie offer, and the producer wanted the ship in Auckland for the filming. I left most of my things—photos, letters and clothes, on board as I planned to unite with *Sofia* in Auckland when the albacore season was over.

Sofia never made it. She sank in a bad storm off the northern-most tip of the North Island of New Zealand, Cape Reinga. One woman drowned when the ship went down. The sixteen survivors were at sea in two life rafts for five days. They were finally rescued by a passing Russian freighter, which saw their last flare.

I was at sea fishing when notified of the sinking. The boat I was on took me back to shore, and I flew to meet the *Sofia* crew in Wellington. I was distraught and felt great personal loss. All my plans had just sunk, along with an innocent young woman and a beautiful ship, in the snap of a finger. I wasn't sure what to do next. My goal had been to go around the world on *Sofia*, and now that plan was history. My visa, along with other *Sofia* crew members', had expired. I had nothing left but the clothes I had taken fishing and a few odds and ends. I decided to go home to San Diego and regroup. I had been out of the country for three years.

So, I guess I did look back, like I'm looking back right now. If Richard were like Fred I wouldn't be here. But Richard makes it worth being anywhere, even right here on *Hazana* pounding into the wind.

On the fifth day, *Hazana* plowed the seas under genny and mizzen, making six knots. The constant rolling from the northeast winds robbed us of our sleep. Our bodies were tense from the fittings clattering, the sails snapping and the rough ride.

The next day brought a reprieve. The wind came around to our beam and pushed us easterly, which is exactly what we needed. Richard wrote "**Bliss**" in the logbook. We decided to ease the sails and run off a little.

Basking in the sun, I twirled the lover's knot ring Richard had made me. Looking across the cockpit, I let my eyes wander over his muscular body. I admired his topaz-colored hair, wavy like the sea, and his short-cropped full beard, bleached gold from the sun.

The next day, Richard said, "I have given up any illusions that the southeast trades will ever do better than east!" We were now under a double reefed main. Richard wrote, "**Flying 6 KTs.**"

The Brooks & Gatehouse wind indicator gave out on Day Eight.

"I can't figure out why all this bloody equipment is breaking down," Richard complained.

"Could it be corrosion, or . . .?"

"Sod, corrosion. It's bloody hi-tech electronics. The sun may not shine every day, but when it does at least it will tell you exactly where you are."

"Then sod bloody hi-tech electronics!" I teased, slapping my palm on the seat locker.

For the next three days *Hazana* flew. The full sails reflected the salmon-colored sun, and we enjoyed reading and relaxing, and getting some much needed sleep.

Sunday, October 2, Day Eleven on *Hazana*, was special for Richard and me. At dusk, phosphorescence sparkled in the turquoise sea. We opened a bottle of wine and toasted our crossing the equator that day and entering the northern hemisphere.

Ahead of us shot a geyser of silver and translucent green spray:

A large pod of pilot whales was coming to play with *Hazana*. We connected the self-steering vane and went to the bow to watch them leap and sing their high-pitched greeting. Grasping the stainless steel pulpit, Richard leaned against my back, his bearded cheek next to mine as the whales created beautiful crisscrossing streamers of chartreuse in front of us.

"Aren't the whales magical, love?" He asked, fascinated.

"Look how they surface and dive," he said as he slowly started undulating against my backside. As *Hazana* rose over the next swell, he whispered in my ear, "Surface . . ." And as the bow plunged into the trough, he said, "Dive."

"You could be a whale, Richard," I teased.

"I am a whale, love. See, I'm surfacing"—he nudged me forward, the rhythm of the whales sparking something amorous in him—"and now I'm going to dive."

As *Hazana* glided down into the trough, Richard reached around and untied my pareu as he clung onto me with his knees. He knotted the material onto the pulpit with a ring knot and cupped my breasts with his warm hands. I let go of the bow pulpit and stretched my arms out wide, *Hazana*'s fair figurehead.

"Ummm," I hummed.

"I want to dive with you, Tami," Richard murmured in my ear. "I want to surface and dive as these wild mammals do." I reached back and undid his shorts. They fell onto the teak deck.

With growing momentum we surfaced and dived, surfaced and dived, wild and free like the whales, before God, and heaven, and sky. *Hazana*, the queen whale, set the rolling rhythm we matched. "Bliss" I later wrote in the logbook.

Day Twelve, we hoisted the multi-purpose sail, the MPS, a very lightweight sail, and made four knots with the southeast trades finally catching us. The trades stayed with us for a number of days, pushing us to the east. We often saw whales, and now dolphins were showing their cheerful faces.

Dawn of October 8 broke gray, rainy and miserable. The winds were unpredictable. They gusted from southeast to southwest and back around from the north. We were up near the bow checking the rig when a small land-bird crashed onto the foredeck. The poor thing panted, unsteady on its short toothpick legs. Richard got a towel and dropped it over the bird. Scooping it up, he brought the bird to the cockpit, out of the rain and wind. Behind the windscreen, on top of the roof of the cabin, it squatted low, ruffling its wet feathers to warm its tired body. I crumbled a piece of bread, but the bird appeared too afraid to eat. The absurd winds must have blown the tiny bird far offshore. Richard later scribbled, "Cyclonic?" in the logbook.

The next day the weather channel WWV informed us the storm they had been tracking off the coast of Central America was now being classified as Tropical Depression Sonia. They said it was centered at 13°N by 136°W and traveling west at seven knots. That put her over a hundred miles west of us.

WWV also warned of a different tropical storm brewing off the coast of Central America. They were referring to it as "Raymond." In comparing our course, 11°N and 129°W heading north-northeast, to the course Raymond was traveling, 12°N and 107°W and heading west at twelve knots, Richard wrote: "WATCH THIS ONE!"

Near midnight the wind dropped. Then it came around to the east-northeast, which fueled Raymond's fury. We got hit with squalls and rain.

Monday, October 10, the wind veered to the north. At five in the morning, we changed our heading to north-northwest to gain speed. Our goal was to get as far north of Raymond's track as possible.

The wind died down to one to two knots, and we ended up

motoring for four hours. But by noon we had two reefs in the main, the staysail up and a reefed genny, and we were plowing away at five knots to the north-northwest. Tropical Storm Raymond was now at 12°N and 111°W, heading due west. The bird was gone; it had flown the coop.

We decided to fly more sail in an attempt to run north of the oncoming storm. Taut lines, also known as jack lines, ran along each side of the boat from the bow to the stern. This allowed us to clip on the tether of our safety harness while working on the deck. We pushed *Hazana* to her max. There was no choice—we had to get out of the path of the storm.

Richard and I got busy clearing the decks just in case it really got bad; we didn't need heavy objects flying around. We hauled the extra five-gallon jury-jugs of diesel down below and secured them in the head. They were heavy, and it was difficult to move them in the rough seas.

At 0100 the next morning, the genny blew out. It thrashed violently in the wind, its staccato cracks and snaps were deafening. Turning on the engine and engaging the auto-pilot, Richard and I cautiously worked our way up to the mainmast, clipping our safety harness tethers onto the jack line as we went forward. "You slack the . . ."

"WHAT?" I yelled over the wailing wind.

"YOU SLACK THE HALYARD WHEN I GET UP THERE, AND I'LL PULL HER DOWN."

"OKAY," I shouted back.

Richard fought his way to the bow. I was terrified watching him slither forward. Gallons of cold water exploded over the bow on top of him, drenching me too. *Hazana* reared over the rising swells. The ruined sail whipped violently and dangerously in the wind.

Richard couldn't get the sail down. Finally he came back to me.

"SHE WON'T BUDGE. CLEAT OFF THE END OF THE HALYARD, AND COME UP AND HELP ME PULL HER DOWN."

I did as he said and slowly worked myself forward on all fours,

25

ducking my head with each dousing of saltwater. We tugged and pulled on the sail as it volleyed madly in the wind. Finally, after my fingers were blistered from trying to grip the wet sailcloth, the sail came down with a thud, half burying us. We gathered it up quickly and sloppily lashed it down. We then slid the number one jib into the foil, and I tied the sheet—the line—onto the sails clew. I made my way back to the cockpit making sure the line was not fouled.

Richard went to the mainmast, wrapped the halyard around the winch and raised as much of the sail as he could by hand. I crawled back to the mainmast and pulled in the excess line while he cranked on the winch, raising the sail the rest of the way. It flogged furiously, like laundry left on a line in a sudden summer squall. We were afraid this sail would rip too. Once the sail was almost completely hoisted, I slithered as fast as I could back to the cockpit while Richard secured the halyard. I cranked like hell on the winch to bring the sail in. Richard came back to the cockpit and gave me a hand getting the sail trimmed. This sail change took us almost two hours. Richard and I were spent and wet, and we needed to eat. In between sets of swells, I slid open the hatch and hurriedly went down into the cabin.

It was hot inside *Hazana* with all the hatches shut. She was moving like a raft in rapids. What would be simple to prepare, I questioned myself, instant chicken soup? As I set the pot of water on the propane stove to boil, I peeled off my dripping foul weather gear and sat down exhausted on the quarter berth.

Seven hours later, after the horrendous sail change, Raymond was still traveling west at latitude 12°N. Richard scribbled in the logbook: "We're okay." We continued north.

All through the rest of the day, the wind and the size of the swells steadily increased. White water blew off the crests of the waves, creating a constant shower of saltwater spray. The ocean was powdered like white feathers bursting out of a down pillow.

Tropical Storm Raymond was now being classified as a hurricane—Hurricane Raymond.

At 0930 October 11, the forecast put Hurricane Raymond at 12°N and spinning along a west-northwest course. Richard recorded: "WE'RE ON THE FIRING LINE." We packed on all sail. I silently lamented over the useless torn genny; it was a sail we could have really used now because it was larger than the number one jib. Richard told me to alter course to the southwest. If we couldn't situate ourselves above Raymond, maybe we could sneak below it and reach the navigable semicircle of the hurricane in the next twenty-four hours.

At three o'clock that afternoon the updated weather report told us Raymond had altered its direction to west from west-northwest with gusts to 140 knots. The afternoon sunsight gave us a second line of position. This told us we would collide with Raymond if we continued on our southwest heading. We immediately came about and headed northeast, trying to get as far away from Raymond as possible. With a shaky hand Richard inscribed: "ALL WE CAN DO IS PRAY."

Later that night, the spinnaker pole's top fitting broke loose from the mainmast and the pole came crashing down, trailing sideways in the water. Richard and I scrambled to the mainmast trying to save the spinnaker pole. He grabbed it before the force of the water could break the bottom fitting and suck the pole overboard. It took both of us to lash its fifteen feet down on the deck. Creeping back to the cockpit we saw that a portion of the mizzen sail had escaped from its slides and was now whipping frantically in the wind.

"JESUS CHRIST, WHAT'S NEXT?" Richard roared. He stepped out of the cockpit, clipped his safety harness onto the mizzen mast, and released the mizzen halyard. Once the mizzen was down, he lashed it onto the mizzen boom.

As he came back to me at the wheel, I noticed how dark the shadows were under his eyes. He tried not to sound sarcastic as he said, "Not much else can go wrong."

Where the ocean was once black at night, it was now

highlighted with thick white caps of foam. The barometer dropped way down the scale as the wind's wail steadily increased, the seas becoming even steeper, angrier, more aggressive. We were terrified Raymond was catching us, but there wasn't a damn thing we could do about it but sail and motor as fast and as hard as possible.

We stayed on watch, taking turns going below to get whatever rest we could. Our muscles ached from fighting the wheel while trying to negotiate the pounding, erratic seas. Night had never lasted so long.

The next morning broke cinder gray with spotty sunlight shedding an overcast hue on brothy seas. Ocean spray slapped us constantly in the face. Wind was a steady forty knots. We were forced to take all sail down and gallop with bare poles.

About 0900 the seas arched into skyscrapers looming over our tiny boat. The anemometer now read a steady fifty knots. The churning spray was ceaseless. Richard came topside and handed me the EPIRB (emergency position-indicating radio device), as he took the wheel. "Here, I want you to put this on."

"What about you?"

"Tami, if we had two I'd put one on. Just make me feel better, and put the bloody thing on."

So, I did. I fastened my safety harness tether to the binnacle and steered while Richard went below to try to figure out our location now and get an updated position of the hurricane. All he could hear between the pounding and screech of the wind was static. There was no way he could risk bringing the radio outside with the sea constantly cascading over the boat.

Richard came topside, fastened his safety harness and took the wheel. I sat huddled against the cockpit coaming, holding on with all my strength to the cleat where my tether was fastened. We were helpless while staring at the raging scene around us. The sound of the screaming wind was unnerving. The hull raised to dizzying heights and dove into chasms. Could the seas swallow us? The ascent of the boat over the monstrous waves sent the hull airborne into a free fall that smashed down with a shutter. I was horrified *Hazana* would split wide open. Finally I shouted to Richard, "IS THIS IT? CAN IT GET ANY WORSE?"

"NO. HANG ON, LOVE; BE MY BRAVE GIRL. SOMEDAY WE'LL TELL OUR GRANDCHILDREN HOW WE SURVIVED HURRICANE RAYMOND."

"IF WE SURVIVE," I hollered back.

"WE WILL. GO BELOW AND TRY TO REST."

"WHAT HAPPENS IF WE ROLL OVER? I DON'T WANT TO LEAVE YOU ALONE."

"THE BOAT WOULD RIGHT ITSELF. LOOK, I'M SECURE," he said, giving a sharp tug on his tether. "I'D COME RIGHT BACK UP WITH IT."

I looked at his tether secured to the cleat on the cockpit coaming.

"GO BELOW" he urged. "KEEP YOUR EYE ON THE BAROMETER. LET ME KNOW THE MINUTE IT STARTS RISING."

Reluctantly I got up, leaned out and squeezed the back of Richard's hand. The wind sounded like jet engines being thrown in reverse.

"HOLD ON," he yelled and cranked the wheel. I tumbled sideways as the hull was knocked down. I fell against the cockpit coaming. An avalanche of white water hit us. The boat shuttered.

Richard anxiously glanced at me, water dripping down his face. Fear jumped out of his intense blue eyes. Behind him rose sheer cliffs of white water, the tops blown into clouds of spray by the ferocious wind. My eyes questioned his—I couldn't hide my terror. He faltered, and then winked at me, thrusting his chin up, a signal for me to go below. His forced grin and lingering eye contact disappeared as I slammed the hatch shut.

I clung to the grab rail of the companionway ladder as I made my way down to the cabin below. The frenzied cadence of *Hazana*'s motion prevented me from doing anything but collapsing into the settee's hammock. I automatically secured the tether of my safety harness around the table's post. I looked up at the ship's clock: It was 1240 hours. My eyes dropped to the barometer: It was terrifyingly low—below twenty-eight inches. Dread engulfed me. I hugged the musty blanket to my chest as I was flung side to side in the hammock. No sooner had I closed my eyes, when all motion stopped. Something felt very wrong, it became too quiet—this trough too deep.

"OHMIGOD," I heard Richard scream.

My eyes popped open. *WHOMP!* I covered my head as I sailed into oblivion.

Chapter Two

1300 to 1600 Hours

"Tami? Tami, its Bridget, boy do I have a gig for you."
"Good, I need a break," I said into the phone. "Where to this time?" I asked feeling my heart pound a little faster.

Bridget always thought of me first when she had to turn down a boat delivery job. This one she said, involved a racing sloop, state of the art, bound for the Big Boat Series at the Saint Francis Yacht Club in San Francisco.

The skipper, a South African named Eric, called me soon thereafter, and we arranged to meet at a local restaurant called the Red Sails to discuss the details of the delivery.

When I walked into the restaurant I spotted Eric by the description he had given me over the phone: "Tall, dark and handsome." I thought he was joking, but it was true. Eric was sitting with two other guys, and I walked up and introduced myself. They had been there for a while and were almost finished eating.

Eric introduced me to Dan, the American, and Richard, the Brit.

I had seen Richard just the day before as he walked through the boat yard. I remembered how I stopped working just to watch him. He was gorgeous. Walking evenly with his lion-like gait and his blond, sun-streaked hair flowing. I had asked my co-worker, Debbie, if she knew who he was. She didn't, but knew he was working on one of the expensive yachts in the yard.

Now I sat down across the table from him. His striking eyes were not exactly baby blue, but darker—lapis lazuli. They caught my attention, and I felt if I stared long enough into them I would find something magic. I didn't want to look away, but did, to respond to a question Eric asked me. "I've sailed from California, all through the South Pacific to New Zealand," I answered.

As Richard took a last bite of his omelet, I noticed his hands were rough, calloused. He ate the European way with the fork upside down in his left hand and the knife in his right hand.

The delivery crew would be Eric, Dan and me, if I decided to take the job. I was disappointed to learn Richard wouldn't be going. He had a work deadline to meet.

As we talked about the delivery, my green eyes would wander to Richard's blue ones and discover them looking at me. As the conversation wound down, in walked a petite, blond woman about thirty. She came up behind Richard and put her hand on his back. I was crushed. I could tell he was attracted to me, but he was obviously taken. What was he doing flirting with me? Damn, I hated to be led on.

Her name was Lizzie, and she had a British accent too. She had come to deliver a message to Richard about work. I watched as Richard and Lizzie left together and hoped my disappointment didn't show. Eric, Dan, and I made plans for the departure of the delivery cruise which would be in five days.

Delivering the boat was a piece of cake. Even rounding notorious Point Conception the water was flat calm. I was rather discouraged because I had been eager to sail this hotshot racing sloop, having never sailed with hydraulics before, let alone a stowaway mainsail. Dan and Eric turned out to be really charming guys: Dan's sense of humor kept us laughing, and Eric's deadpan demeanor and boating skills kept us on track.

The elite St. Francis Yacht Club was right on the bay in downtown San Francisco. The location was spectacular, but the ambiance was unwelcoming—I felt out of it. The club was overrun by beauties wearing the latest fashion in boating attire. Hiding my insecurities, I walked into one of the bars at the club and sat down. The waiter came up to me and said, "Excuse me, ma'am, this is a gentleman's bar."

"A gentleman's bar?" I asked. "What does that mean?"

"It means men only, no women."

"You've got to be kidding." I looked around at all these men staring at me.

"On the contrary," declared the waiter.

"Well, if men would rather entertain men . . ." I stated matter of factly as I pushed my chair back, stood up with a deep breath and sauntered slowly out of the bar trying to imitate a model strutting down the runway.

Through overheard conversations and a few conversations of my own, it didn't take long to figure out I had probably clocked more blue water nautical miles than seventy-five percent of the sailors there. I mused over the amount of money people spent on trinkets like diamonds rings, earrings and pendants. The fancy gold-braided replicas of nautical symbols must have cost a fortune. Rolexes were on practically every wrist. It's a wonder the mirror in the ladies room didn't break from all the jealous glaring going on. It was obvious the competition wasn't just on the water. It didn't take me long to realize these racing sled-type yachts and the accompanying lifestyle weren't for me.

During the entire week of the delivery, I hadn't been able to get Richard off my mind. I subtly asked Dan questions about Richard and learned that he was thirty-four years old and that his relationship with Lizzie was on the rocks. Dan told me Richard had built his sailboat in South Africa and was circumnavigating the world when he decided to make a brief stop in San Diego to do a few repairs and earn a few bucks. This information piqued my interest again.

With the delivery over, Dan and I flew home. Dan was between jobs, so I hired him to help me in my brightwork business. I had a large job starting on my return.

About a week after we returned from the delivery, Richard came by and asked Dan and I to join him for lunch. I stashed my brown bag and said sure as casually as possible. I was swooning. I felt his eyes on me as I climbed down the ladder. He reached out and took my elbow as I stepped off the bottom rung. What a gentleman. My heart was caught—hook, line and sinker.

I started spending more time with Dan, his wife, Sandra, Eric and Richard. Occasionally Lizzie showed up. She was pleasant enough, easy to like; however, I could see Richard's mood change when she arrived and they would soon end up leaving together.

One afternoon Richard came by the boat I was varnishing and asked me to have dinner with him that night. I hesitated and then told him I would be uncomfortable spending time with him while he was with Lizzie. He said he was asking me to dinner so he could explain his relationship with her, and so we could talk about the South Pacific. He would be sailing there next year, without her, and he'd love to pick my brain about it in a peaceful setting—like a quiet restaurant. I thought about saying no, but after all, I did know a lot about the South Pacific. And how could I say no when my heart was sending a Morse code "Y-E-S." I agreed to have dinner with him later that night.

I called my mom that day, and the conversation led to my planned rendezvous with Richard. I wanted her to meet him. I also wanted to hear about the latest in her love life. She lived nearby,

My mother and I

so we agreed to meet around six and have a drink at the restaurant before he arrived.

Richard found us in the bar, and I introduced them. I could tell he was surprised she was my mother and not my sister. After all, my mom and Richard were closer in age than he and I were. When he glanced away, my mom gave me an approving "He's a doll!" look. I'm sure he sensed some silent message being passed between us, because when he looked back, Mom and I froze, stone-faced. His eyes were questioning mine when Lizzie walked in. She acted polite, yet irritated and asked Richard for a word—alone. He excused himself. I felt confused.

"Take it easy, honey," my mom calmly said, realizing right away that Richard had some excess baggage.

"He swears they're as good as broken up."

"Don't jump to any conclusions; just wait and hear what he has to say. He didn't look too happy to see her."

"Excuse me," my mom said to the bartender, "two of the same, please."

It wasn't long before Richard returned. Mom took one last sip and graciously made an exit. Richard and I were shown to our table. My nerves were tight.

Richard explained he and Lizzie had split up but that she was still living on his boat while she made plans to return to England. He said that after meeting me he'd finally had enough of keeping his life and feelings on hold. After I had accepted his dinner invitation, he told her about it. She didn't like it, he confessed, but he explained to her he was ready to get on with his life and she should get on with hers. He apologized for her showing up and hoped it didn't embarrass me. The electricity between us, I'm sure, could be felt throughout the restaurant.

I felt much better, actually greatly relieved, that he would soon not be entangled with anyone. We had a wonderful evening and learned a lot about each other. He was an only child, with a step-sister, Susie, thirteen years older than he. I told him about my family. But, more importantly, we learned of each other's great passion for the sea.

Richard had been born in England, in 1949, to an upper-middle-class family. His father was a retired navy man who did well after the war. His mother, he sadly confessed, had committed suicide when he was seven. His father soon remarried, and Richard thought of his stepmother as his "Mum".

He was enrolled in the Naval Academy near London to be prepped as an officer in the Navy. But once of age, he started to rebel against his father's wishes and got kicked out of the academy. He finished his schooling in another private school, but felt his father had never forgiven him for going against his wishes.

After Richard graduated, he went to work for Olivetti, a manufacturing and sales company for electronic office equipment. He was good at sales and ended up buying a flat in London. He gathered a fine wardrobe and went through a few racy cars. (And a few racy women too, I'm sure.) But with a faraway look in his eyes, he admitted he had still felt unfulfilled. When a position in the company opened up in South Africa, Richard grabbed it. He adjusted quickly to South Africa and began to thrive on its beauty and diversity. But he despised apartheid, which inhibited his ability to socialize with anyone he pleased.

While with Olivetti, Richard met a man at a boat yard that built ferro-cement boats. They became fast friends, and soon Richard was offered a partnership in the yard. He eagerly took the job, quitting Olivetti with no regret. He loved being involved in building the thirty to fifty-foot yachts. It was at this point that Richard met Eric, the skipper who had hired me to help deliver the racing sailboat to San Francisco.

I felt this was an opportune time to throw a tack in our conversation, so I asked him about his love life. Richard explained that he had married a South African woman, Caroline, and that they had planned to build their dream boat and sail around the world. But by the time the boat, *Mayaluga*, was finished, their marriage was rocky. On the shakedown cruise, Caroline got deathly seasick. They agreed Richard would continue with the boat to the Caribbean, and she would follow. Later, when she didn't show up, Richard flew back to South Africa, where Caroline was pursuing a career in publishing. He tried to talk her into staying committed to their marriage but it was to no avail. The marriage ended in divorce. That had been over two years ago.

I asked when Lizzie had come into the picture. Richard said he had met her in the Caribbean while he was waiting out the hurricane season. They hit it off, and Lizzie had decided to sail to San Diego with him. He had chosen San Diego after receiving a letter from Eric telling him what a great place it was to winter-over. Richard was also told he could prepare his boat for the South Pacific there and, with his skills, could easily find work on boats.

If Richard could have read my mind just then, he would have heard me thinking, *you came here because you were meant to find me.*

Richard totally captured my attention when those blue, blue eyes penetrated mine and he confessed Lizzie just wasn't the one—they weren't cut from the same cloth. He was born to see the world, and nothing—nobody—would stop him. There was no doubt he wanted me to know this right from the start.

I wondered what his plans would be after he'd sailed around

Richard at the helm of Mayaluga

the world. Would he just keep going around and around? I found a subtle way of asking this, and he said he didn't know for sure, but thought he would like to have a family one day. Maybe he'd even buy the little boat yard he'd seen in the south of England, if it went up for sale. But first, the South Pacific. He asked somewhat cavalierly, whether I would like to go with him.

I laughed, but deep down inside, I tingled. *Was he serious?* "It's late; we need to slow down," I said, even though one part of me wanted to jump on his boat and leave for the South Pacific that night.

When we walked to my car, he leaned over and gave me a light kiss good night. It was like heaven, but hell too. I was dying to abandon all "good girl" protocol and throw my arms around him and never let him go. But, to my dismay, the sensible side of me won out, as it usually does. Lizzie needed to be out of his life before I could let myself in.

As I drove home I was smiling from ear to ear. I had never felt this way about any man before. He aroused latent dreams in me. I knew then and there I was going to the South Pacific.

About a week later, Richard told me that his grandmother had passed away in England, and he needed to go home for the funeral. Lizzie would be on the same flight. I felt he was trying to tell me it was over between us. Clenching my fists, I politely offered my condolences, turned around and walked away. He caught up to me and explained Lizzie was going home to England and not returning to America, but he would be back soon. As Richard said good-bye to me, he said, "Tami, now that I've found you, I'll never let you go." He was so direct, I melted into his arms. We kissed passionately. I could have died and gone to heaven—with his grandma!

Chapter Three

Coming To

I opened my eyes. The thought, "I could have died and gone to heaven," hazily lingered in my mind. My head throbbed. I went to touch it, but things, I didn't know what, lay on top of me, smothering me, crushing me. What was going on here? I couldn't think, I couldn't remember. Where was I? My hammock hung cockeyed. I dangled near the floor. A can of WD-40 clanged against the table post. I moved, and a book splashed into the water sloshing about the cabin sole.

I struggled to free myself. Dead weight pinned me down. Cans of food, books, pillows, clothes, and panels of the main saloon's overhead liner spilled off of me. Covered in blood, I could feel a horrendous cut on my left shin.

Where was I? What had happened? I was confused. I couldn't orient myself. My tether, still clipped onto the table post, confined me. I was obviously on a boat—what boat? My weakened hands frantically tried to unclip the tether.

Once unclipped, I strained to see around me. My vision was blurry; the pain in my head, excruciating. Putting hand to brow, I flinched, "Ouch!" I looked at my hand and saw crimson. Uncontrollable shivers engulfed me.

Laboriously, I crawled out of the labyrinth of wreckage and stared. The interior of the boat was chaotic. My God, what had happened? Books, charts, pillows, spoons, floorboards, cups, clothing, cans of food, spare parts, beans, flour, oatmeal—everything was either floating or stuck to the overhead, or to the bulkheads, or to the hull. What boat is this? Where am I?

The oven had been ripped from the starboard side of the boat and was now wedged into the nav station bookshelf on the port side. I gazed intently at the ship's clock, but I couldn't bring the numbers into focus.

Unsteadily, I stood up, my knees wobbling. I felt faint. Slowly, one careful step at a time, I negotiated my way through the obstacles floating in the four inches of water that lapped above the floorboards. I got to the ship's clock and watched its second hand jump: one thousand one, one thousand two. It read 1600 hours, 4 p.m. Wait. Hadn't it been just about 1 p.m. . . . ?

I headed for the V-berth. "Hello?" I called out. My voice sounded strange. I gaped at the turmoil in every nook and cranny. Cautiously moving toward the bow, I peeked in the head. There, in the mirror, stood a frazzled image, its face covered in blood, the forehead cut wide open. Long strands of hair, wild and matted with blood, shot out from its skull. In fear, my hands flew to my mouth. I screamed. Then I screamed again. The ungodly sight was me.

"No!" I shouted and crashed into the bulkhead as I tried to escape.

I stumbled into the V-berth. Everything there too was jumbled—topsy-turvy. The storage hammocks that hung on each side of the berth were overturned; spilled clothes lay every which way. Paperback books were off their shelves. The long mattress for the bunk was kinked, out of its place. Cans of food and even broken dishes lay strewn about.

I shook my head and wondered how the food and dishes got in the V-berth. In disbelief I backed into the main salon.

"Ray?" I apprehensively called.

Ray? I wondered where that had come from. It's not Ray. Ray's the hurricane. Hurricane? Hurricane Ray—Raymond. Where's Richard? Richard . . . "Oh my God . . ." But that's what he said . . .

Fear dropped me to my knees. I retched. Bilge water splashed against my cheek. Richard had not come below with me.

"RICHARD?" I screamed. "RICHAAARRRD."

I pulled myself to my feet, but had barely taken a step when the heel of my foul weather boot slid. I fell against the saloon table. I threw- up again.

"RICHAAARRRD?" I screamed as I crawled toward the companionway ladder, my hands splashing water in every direction as I knocked food, tools, books, whatever, out of my way.

"RICHARD? RICHARD?" I screamed over and over, choking on my words.

The companionway ladder had broken off its latches, and it lay sideways against the nav station seat. I pushed it to the floor, out of my way, and climbed up on the back of the settee, screaming Richard's name. I hoisted myself up into the cockpit. It was difficult. I had no strength.

The boom blocked the companionway. "Goddamn it!" I wailed and then painfully climbed over it.

Desperately I looked in every direction. Richard was nowhere to be seen.

Hazana was ravaged. The main mast was gone except for a four foot piece still attached to the main boom. The tabernacle, a metal housing used to raise and lower the main mast, lay on its side, a huge four-foot-piece of torn deck attached to it. The large two-inch clevis pin that had been holding the foot of the mast into the tabernacle lay on the deck, sheered in half. "Oh my God," I wailed as I looked down through the gaping hole on deck into the main cabin. The mizzen mast was in the water only holding on by the starboard shroud. Stainless steel rigging hung overboard, with the roller-furling jib and staysail trailing in the water. Only a couple of stainless steel one-inch stanchions were left standing, tweaked like pop cans. The rest of the stanchions, and their lifelines, were gone. The propane-locker hatch was missing, and the propane tanks were gone.

"MY GOD . . . RICHARD? RICHARD?" I howled.

I looked all around. "Richard? Richard?"

Oh please, God, please. My legs gave way—I hung onto the boom and retched again.

He couldn't be gone. The dry heaves choked me. In total fear, I grabbed the boom and lay dazed, my cheek against the cold aluminum.

"Get up. Move." An inner voice slammed into my thoughts.

Bawling, I crept over the broken-down boom, reached into the companionway and groped for the binoculars. Miraculously, they were still strapped in their place.

After slithering back over the boom, I stood bracing myself, thinking, "I can save him, I can save him," as I scanned the ocean around me with the binoculars. I could not stop trembling: The eye holes of the magnifying glasses pressed hard against my skull—drumming against my eyebrows.

I peered in every direction. All I saw was a vast desolate sea, with rolling four-foot swells. Nothing, not one goddamned thing, was out there.

"Try the engine!" the inner voice barked.

I pulled out the choke, adjusted the throttle and pushed the engine's start button. Nothing. Not even a grunt or grind.

I looked toward the wheel. There I saw Richard's safety line secured to the cleat on the cockpit coaming. The tether hung over the side of the hull. My God, could he be on the other end?

I lunged for the safety line, grabbed it tight and yanked hard. It flew into the cockpit, the metal making a sharp, cracking sound against the fiberglass. There lay the bitter end—the D-ring—parted.

I became a lunatic. Forcing the seat lockers open, I threw cushions, anything that would float, overboard. He's out there somewhere. Maybe he's alive. Oh God, please . . .

"Take this. And this. And this . . . Hold on Richard, I'll find you."

I clambered below and grabbed more cushions, pushing them up through the main hatch. Crawling back topside, I heaved it all overboard. The debris undulated in the otherwise empty sea. Adrenaline raced through my body causing my heart to pound furiously.

Spotting the man-overboard pole attached to the mangled stern rail, I raced to the stern and struggled desperately to get the pole untied. I threw it as far out in the sea as I could. The orange flag bobbed in the swells.

He could be alive, it's only been three hours.

His last words, "Ohmigod," roared in my brain. It must have been a huge wave. Larger than those forty-five-foot monsters. A rogue wave. We rolled, and Richard . . . Oh, my love . . . God, you wouldn't—you couldn't . . .

I started dry heaving all over again. I hugged my convulsing stomach and felt the EPIRB still attached to my waist. I fumbled to unbuckle it. I couldn't center my mind. How does this thing work?

Remove the guard. Press the switch. Nothing. I stood up and held the radio device in the air. Nothing. I turned it in circles. Nothing. I sat down and started over.

I put the guard back on and then took it off. I pressed the switch and held the EPIRB up. Fumbling, I pulled out the batteries. With trembling fingers I wiped off the connectors and then put everything back together. Nothing. Damn it!

Water. The EPIRB needs water. Yanking open the seat locker I could see the bucket lying deep in the hole. It was the bucket Richard and I had used to pour saltwater over each other to cool off. Stretching, I grabbed the line on the bucket.

Holding the stern rail I threw the bucket into the water, scooped up as much saltwater as I could lift and heaved the bucket into the cockpit. I dropped the EPIRB in it. Bubbles rose, but nothing else happened. No lights or beeps. I yanked the EPIRB out of the water and shook it. Nothing. Disgusted, I threw it back in the bucket. Saltwater splashed all over, burning the deep cut on my shin.

I couldn't think clearly. My head throbbed and my body ached with every movement. There was nothing else I could think to do, short of jumping overboard and ending this nightmare. If Richard had beckoned, I would have jumped.

"Don't, he could be alive."

"How in the hell can he be alive?" I shouted to no one.

Defeat and exhaustion engulfed me. I couldn't bear to look at the reality of the situation any longer. I crawled below.

Chapter Four

Sinking

I stepped down into a deep puddle. A good four inches of water covered the cabin sole. I gasped and thought, my God the boat's sinking, I've gotta get out of here. I went to the companionway and hoisted myself out. Frantically I struggled to move the heavy life raft to the side deck where I secured it to the cabin-top hand-rail. Instinctively I grabbed the rigging knife I kept on my belt and slid the sharp blade under a strap that held the raft shut and started cutting upward. It was too tough—I was too weak. So, I resorted to hacking away at the straps.

As the last strap split, the life raft inflated as it flung open. Inside I found fishing gear, hand flares, a miniature medical kit and cans of water. Something was wrong, something was miss-ing. I tried to think, fishing gear, flares, medical kit, food and water. Food? There's no food. There's cans of water but no opener for the cans. How can a life raft have no food and no way to open the water? I flashed in disbelief.

Going back over the boom, I banged the deep gash on my left shin. It started bleeding again. I ignored it. It was nothing compared to . . .

I went below to get food. Wading through the river, kicking everything in my way aside, I picked up a duffel bag. Grabbing biscuits, cans of beans, tuna and peaches, I threw them into the bag. I took hold of the portable world band radio receiver and a can opener, and threw them in too. I pushed a blanket and a pil-low out the companionway into the cockpit.

Water. I must have more water.

I looked around and saw the solar shower bag dangling from a shelf. It could hold two and a half gallons of water. "Richard will be thirsty when I find him," I said out loud. Grabbing the bag I took it to the galley and began to fill it using the pressurized fresh water system. As the bag was filling, the stream of water started slowing down. It became a sputter, then a spit. "My God, I don't have any water!" Wait—the water filter's canister; there's bound to be at least a half gallon of water in it.

I pushed in the solar bag's stopper and struggled to get the heavy bag out the companionway. Slipping back down to the cabin sole, I took hold of the now-full duffel bag and fought to get it topside. It weighed a ton, it tapped every ounce of strength I had.

I loaded the duffel bag into the life raft and then the bedding. As I was grabbing the solar bag, a swell hit *Hazana* broadside, causing her to roll. Everything in the life raft tumbled overboard.

"NOT THE RADIO!" I screamed, as I watched the duffel bag sink and the bedding float away.

I couldn't stand it. I became a raving lunatic, stomping on the cabin sole and kicking at the life raft. "THAT WAS STUPID, STU-PID. I'M SO STUPID. RICHARD, WHERE ARE YOU? YOU COME AND GET ME. DO YOU HEAR ME? YOU COME AND GET ME! GOD, YOU'VE GOT TO HELP ME!"

Wailing with utter frustration, I grabbed the solar bag and crawled inside the life raft, shaking with fear and futility—bab-bling: "I can't take it, Richard, I just can't take it. Why didn't you take me with you? You said, 'The Captain goes down with the ship.' Remember? You said that! You lied to me. The ship did not go down. Where are you? How can I go on without you? What am I supposed to do? I don't know what to do. God, what should I do?"

"You never leave the ship," came Richard's soothing voice. He said it over and over, softly in my head. Hugging the water bag to my chest, I shut my eyes and sobbed, "But you left the ship, you left the ship." I cried myself to sleep in the rubber raft, not caring if the ship and I did sink.

Chapter Five

Currents and Drift

I woke up blubbering and freezing. I tried to open my crusty eyes. My neck and whole body felt stiff. Desperately I wanted to keep sleeping, or die, so I wouldn't have to deal with this nightmare. But the chill from the breeze, the clanging of broken gear, and the slap of water against the hull awoke all my fears again.

Giving up, I grabbed a can of water out of the life raft and went below. At the sink I pumped weak spits of fresh water into my hand, slurped it and then licked my right palm. "Ugh, salty." I spit the saline residue out. Still thirsty, I opened the can of water I had brought below and drank it all. It made me dizzy, it tasted horrible. All I wanted to do was lie back down and sleep until this horror went away.

Once in the aft-cabin I swiped the books and clothes out of my way and then collapsed on the berth, shivering. I pulled a towel and some T-shirts over me and curled up in a ball, hugging Richard's broken guitar. There was a big hole in it. He would have hated that.

I woke up later to a door banging. I had been dreaming I was at a Victorian ball, dressed in a beautiful billowing affair, as were all the women. The men were in fancy costumes too. Renaissance-type music and long tables of food filled the room. The lighting had a yellow glow like candlelight, only brighter. Everyone was happy and gay, dancing around eating and drinking. It was wonderful.

The door banged again. I yelled: "RICHARD, GET THE DOOR." My heart froze. Oh, Richard, come back, please, come back. Richard. . .

I lay there and cried all over again. How could this happen?

Why? We were so happy . . . I started coughing and spit up blood. Oh God, what does this blood mean? Engulfed in loneliness and depression, I pretended Richard was there in the berth with me and I hugged the guitar tighter. I closed my eyes. The rise and fall of *Hazana* over the swells reminded me of riding the manta rays.

I kept my eyes squeezed shut and let myself reminisce about the good times: Remember riding the manta rays, Richard?

We anchored *Mayaluga* in Hakahetau Bay, on Ua Pou of the Marquesas Islands. A local named Luk invited us to go shark diving with him and some of his friends that night. I wasn't thrilled about the idea of shark diving, but not wanting to be left behind, I decided to go and just stay in the outrigger while the others dived.

Five of us went in two outriggers. The guys were using masks and snorkels, not air tanks, so they couldn't dive too deep or stay underwater too long. I saw Luk motion to Richard, and they both went down at the same time. All of a sudden I noticed their flashlights speed by, under the outrigger and beyond. After a few seconds, the lights headed for the surface, and Richard came bolting out of the water with Luk right behind him. I thought for sure a great white shark was on their tails. Swimming over to me Richard shouted, "You have to try this, love—we just rode a manta ray!"

Being content and safe in the outrigger, there was no way I was going in that shark-infested water. But after about a half-hour of watching the guys have the time of their lives, I thought, why not. I called Richard over and told him I was ready to try.

My stomach rose to my throat as I slid into the

Hakahetau Bay, Ua Pou, Marquesas

warm water. Richard and Luk swam over, and Luk motioned for me to stay close to him. Luk dove, and I dove right behind him. Below us was a huge black manta ray. Luk grabbed onto its fin, I grabbed onto Luk's leg, and off we went.

When I couldn't hold my breath any longer, I let go and watched Luk's light zip ahead as the manta swam away with its human cargo. Briefly alone, treading water, I turned my flashlight down toward the ocean floor. I could see nothing but my legs kicking. I looked up at the sky. The stars were brilliant. A "whoop," then a light shining into my face drew my attention.

"What are you doing, love?" Richard asked.

"Nothing, just catching my breath."

In the couple of hours we spent manta surfing, I was able to grab onto only one manta ray by myself and ride. I was apprehensive because I knew that the six-foot wing span could knock me silly unless the large ray was gliding as I grabbed hold. The blade along the shoulder was firm, but the skin felt slimy and slick. I began to realize that these creatures were like pets to our new friends and that manta surfing was something our friends must have learned to do as teens.

Later Luk explained that manta rays are different from stingrays. Mantas are also known as devil rays. They are the largest of the rays and like to bask on the surface of the sea rather than live on the ocean floor like the sting ray. Luk said mantas like to play and leap in the air.

I was relieved we never saw any sharks that night. We returned to *Mayaluga* totally exhausted, and I dreamed a manta ray befriended us, swimming alongside the boat escorting us as we sailed through the islands.

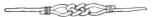

I woke up from my dream of manta ray riding drenched with perspiration. It was as if I had been out riding a ray. My damp foul weather gear clung to my body. The air in the berth was dank. Condensation ran down the hull. The water on the cabin sole lapped to *Hazana*'s rolling motion. The rhythmic banging and creaking wouldn't cease. Finally, I made myself get up.

I sloshed my way into the main salon; nothing had changed. The mess seemed to have grown. The nightmare remained. Stiff and aching all over, I climbed out of the boat and rested in the cockpit. I took hold of the binoculars and searched for Richard again. There was nothing, nothing at all out there but the glare of the sun off the water. Putting the binoculars down I leaned back and let the sun's warmth caress me. I wanted more warmth. With a mighty effort I peeled off my wet clothes. As each piece of clothing dropped off, the sun felt warmer and warmer, melting the icy crypt I was frozen in. How can this feel so good when I feel so bad? It just didn't make sense.

I dozed until a fresh breeze woke me. I stared out to sea for a long time. The gleaming ocean tried to persuade me to be its friend again. I hate you flashed through my mind.

Turning and looking behind me, I saw nothing but a vast sheet of turquoise bleeding into a endless cobalt blue sky. No clouds, no white caps, no monstrous seas, no Richard. Just the sea and me.

I had to move. This was no good. There was so much I should be doing. Why was I alive? What did I live for? This? What is this? A test? A test for what? Endurance? Torture? Had I been greedy in wanting all life has to offer? In wanting Richard? No. This is something else. What? I didn't know. God, what is this? Why?

Anxiety made me start shaking all over again. Take a deep breath I told myself. Feel the sun. I laid down and let the sun hit as much of my nude body as it could. I dozed, eventually waking up hot, covered with sweat.

"You need to get the water out of the boat." The thought didn't force itself into my brain; it drifted in slowly, waiting to see if I'd accept it. I did. I got up and went into the dungeon.

It stunk. The beautiful tangerine and royal blue pareu Richard had bought me in Tahiti lay tangled in the hammock; I freed it and wrapped it around me. I stood there looking around, not knowing what to do.

"You need to get the water out of the boat," said the voice in

my mind again. I obeyed. I went over to the nav station and turned on the bilge-pump switch. Nothing happened. I knelt down and put my hand in the bilge water, thinking maybe I could feel if the external float switch had been fouled by some debris. As I touched it I got shocked. "OUCH!" I pulled my hand away. But if it was getting juice . . . I tentatively touched it once more and got zapped again.

I resorted to the manual bilge pump, but with all the debris in the water, its screen fouled quickly. I didn't have the strength to deal with it and gave up. Resting against a settee I stewed over the big job ahead—to get all this water out of the boat. As *Hazana* didn't appear to be taking on any more water, I could slow down I told myself—deal with it a little at a time.

Suddenly I noticed the exposed molded fiberglass of the cabin's ceiling. The Naugahyde-covered plywood sheets that used to cover the ceiling had fallen down and were strewn about. I got up and went to the V-berth. Digging through my backpack I found my rarely used plum-colored lipstick. Back in the main salon I grabbed the sheets of liner and shoved them topside. I crawled up into the cockpit and wrote on each piece:

HELP—I AM DEMASTED AT 15°N LAT

Each finished laminate was pushed overboard and stiffly undulated in the swells as it drifted with the current further and further away from me. Finally all five signs were cast out to sea, racing to find my rescuer. I would lose sight of them in the troughs, only to catch a glimpse as they crested the swells with their wet white vinyl reflecting my plum-colored plea to the heavens.

What's the point? What's the bloody point? I asked myself dejectedly.

But then that strange little voice in my head, the voice that was becoming my friend, my savior, mysteriously butted in and said: *"Don't give up, love. Don't give up."*

Was it Richard? It didn't sound like Richard.

"You need to get this boat moving," the voice softly hinted.
"Leave me alone."
"Why don't you eat something?"
"Why don't you?"
"Okay, I will."

The voice's invisible hands gently pulled me up by my armpits. I went below. The mess made me nauseous. "Forget it," I said aloud, my voice sounding strange. I headed for the aft-cabin, where I hunted and dug around until I found the big wire cutters. Weak and exhausted, I rested against the berth.

"EAT!" The voice startled me. I looked around uneasily. No one was there. I went back into the main salon. In the galley I saw peanut butter. Even though I didn't feel hungry, I grabbed the jar and tried to open it. I couldn't get the lid off. I knew that voice would scream at me if I didn't try harder, so I banged the lid of the jar on the counter. The sound reverberated in my head. The lid opened. I found a spoon in the upheaval and dug out an oily scoop, setting the open jar on the galley counter.

"Go ahead, fall off, I could care less." I addressed the innocent container of peanut butter: "Why aren't you already broken anyway?" When the jar stayed put, I directed my attention to the manual bilge pump. I strained to give it a couple of pumps, and with food and cutters in hand, I crawled up to the cockpit.

Once topside I had to rest; repeatedly climbing in and out of the boat and carrying the heavy wire-cutters had exhausted me. I licked the peanut butter. It was thick, creamy, not good or bad. All I knew was that it made that strange voice in me happy. Richard loved peanut butter. I wondered what he had found to eat by now.

Sitting there, taking small lick after small lick of peanut butter, I tried to plan a logical order to getting rid of the rigging that dragged in the water. It held *Hazana*'s beam to the swells, causing a very annoying sideways rock. I must hurry in case Richard is starving. I must get to land, he might be waiting for me. With the big wire cutters I started with the mizzen mast. I spent a long time trying to cut free the three-eighth-inch stainless steel shroud. My muscles felt weak and strained. Atrophied. I wanted desperately to quit. But who would do this if I didn't?

With the final cut, *Hazana* straightened and regained some of her composure; but I lost what little I had left when what remained of the mizzen mast sunk. I hoped this was the right thing to do.

"It was the right thing to do. You couldn't lift all that weight on board. It was a hazard bashing into the hull," the voice assured me.

There was still the roller-furling jib and staysail, trailing in the water off the bow. Sails! If only I were strong enough to get them on board. I went to the bow and stared at the sails in the water. There was no way to save the jib, so I finally pulled the clevis pin that was holding it and watched the sail free itself from the staysail and slowly diminish in size as *Hazana* drifted forward with the current.

With nothing to lose, and possibly a lot to gain, I tried to haul in the staysail. It was sopping wet, holding tons of water in its folds. I could barely lift it an inch.

"I can't do it. I just can't." With no winch and no muscle, I gave up and pulled its clevis pin too, then sat down on the deck crying and sobbing as the staysail floated away in the water. I had desperately hoped it would be sailing me to land.

Hazana liked not being encumbered by her fouled rigging and I liked the freshened breeze. Tears weren't solving anything.

Standing up, I staggered back to the cockpit and went below. The nav station was a mess, littered with books and broken glass. I wiped the glass off the seat and sat down. Taking hold of the microphone, I called for help: "Mayday. Mayday. Mayday. Does anybody hear me?" Nothing.

"Damn thing." As I let go of the mike it sprung back across the chart table. Why should I hang it up properly? It was broken like everything else.

Putting my hand to my forehead, I felt the burn from the gash. *"You better look at that cut,"* the voice whispered.

"I don't want to." But I got up and went to the head anyway. It wasn't me I stared at in the mirror, it was some freak. I could see layers of skin inside the deep gash. "My brain is oozing out. Good," I said without much conviction.

I dug the medical kit out from inside the cabinet, and set it down on the closed lid of the commode. As I searched through it, I found a vial of morphine. I picked it up and looked at it mesmerized. Then I looked at the freak in the mirror.

"No, Tami. Don't even think about it," came the voice.

"Why not?" I challenged.

"Because if you were meant to die, you would have."

"I wish I would have."

"I know."

To kill myself would be against everything I had been taught in my life. At least Richard died admirably, doing what he loved, and there was the slight chance he could still be alive.

I carefully put the vial back in the medical bag, placed the bag back in the cabinet and slammed the door shut. Opening the witch hazel I had found, I used it to clean the wound on my forehead. There were sutures on board, but I couldn't bring myself to sew my head together. So, I put several large butterfly bandages on the long wound. Then I carefully rubbed the cuts on my arms and legs with antibacterial ointment. It hurt, but not nearly as much as the thought of how Richard must hurt.

I found a bandanna in the V-berth and pulled my hair up, wrapping the cloth around my head. I had no inclination to deal with my hair or the gash. I leaned against the berth, hating myself for not being able to commit suicide. I didn't know what to do; there was so much to do.

"Check the chart. Make a plan to get to land," ordered the voice.

Begrudgingly, I got up and aimed for the nav station. If I was going to live, let's get to living, so I needed to get going. And maybe, just maybe, Richard would be my reward at the end of this.

At the nav station, I found the chart we used that showed our last known position plotted on it. I forced myself to concentrate as best I could and went over and over the path Richard and I had traveled from Tahiti.

I can't be that far from the accident, can I? I looked at the clock—lets see, I came to what two–three days ago? Two, I think. Glancing down at the chart, I picked up the plotting tools and started to calculate. I decided Cabo San Lucas must be about twelve hundred miles to the northeast, and Hilo, Hawaii, approximately fifteen hundred miles to the northwest. I calculated this repeatedly on the chart. I'll be better off going with the trades and currents to Hawaii. That heading would be about three hundred degrees on the compass.

"But Cabo is closer to home."

I have no home without Richard.

"You have many homes. You have your mom's home and your dad's home. You have your grandma and grandpa's home."

"Is Richard home?"

"Yes, Richard is home. Now, you go home via Hawaii; it makes the most sense."

"What do you mean Richard is home?" Silence. The only sound in my brain was its own buzzing. "WHAT DO YOU MEAN RICHARD IS HOME?" I yelled.

The voice wouldn't answer.

"WELL THEN, GO TO HELL, VOICE," I screamed. To spite the voice I went to the sink, where I cranked the handle on the faucet and waited through each airy sputter as a cup filled with water. Then I drank greedily, even licking the last drops.

"You already had four ounces of water."

"SHUT UP!" I yelled, glancing at the water gauge that read empty. Filled with guilt, I threw the cup down. Going over to a berth I grabbed a sleeping bag, Richard's flowered shirt and his guitar, and pushed it all topside, leaving the morbid dungeon.

Vowing never to go below again, I made a bed in the cockpit and lashed the wheel to keep the rudder straight, which would help *Hazana* make as much headway as possible with the current.

If the sun comes out tomorrow, I can take a sun sight. If the sun comes out.

I started rocking back and forth, back and forth. At some point I picked up Richard's guitar and started strumming and singing.

I put the guitar down and crawled into the sleeping bag, pulling it tightly around me.

"Goodnight, love," I uttered to the star-filled sky.

"Goodnight yourself, love," the voice ever so lightly whispered back.

Chapter Six
Jury Rig

M y face felt on fire. I opened my eyes, only to be blinded by
the sun. "Not another day," I moaned.

"Come on, Tami. Get up. Eat something. Get this boat moving."

The voice was scary, yet comforting too. It always seemed to
know what to do, or what I should do. Actually, it was many
voices. Sometimes it sounded like my mother, or my father, or
my best friend, Mary. But mostly it sounded like Richard.

I went below and got more peanut butter because it was easy.
Back in the sun, I sat sporadically licking my spoon, trying to
figure out how to get *Hazana* moving. The spinnaker pole caught
my eye. It was still lashed down on the foredeck but about six
feet had been sheared off of it when the main mast went over.

The anchor-chain locker was about three feet deep. I unlashed
the nine-foot spinnaker pole and stuck it down in the locker. It
stood only about six feet in the air. "This is ridiculous."

"It's not ridiculous."

"How am I going to fill a sail with wind if the pole's only six
feet in the air?"

"Fill up the chain locker so the pole's higher in the air."

"You fill it up."

"Okay, gladly."

As I laid the pole on the deck to go below, the strange force
establishing itself in me silently directed me to lash the pole back
down. Could the voice be like a guardian angel? That was a weird
thought.

"Why is it a weird thought?"

I don't know . . .

In the V-berth, I opened the hatch and pushed out onto the

bow all the pillows and blankets and anything else that would fill up the chain locker. Then I crawled out of the hatch and shut it behind me.

Into the chain locker I crammed all the objects I had pushed topside. I unlashed the spinnaker pole and then stood it up in the locker. The pole reached a full nine feet into the air. It gave me the first sense of well-being I had felt since I came to. Something was finally being accomplished. I lashed the pole back onto the deck before I went back to the cockpit. I couldn't take the chance of losing the pole overboard.

"You're the last sail I've got," I said aloud to the storm jib. "You're the miracle sail. How did you not get swept overboard? The propane tanks got ripped out of their locker, and the deck's wiped clean, but you stayed in the cockpit without even being tied down. Why didn't Richard? Why didn't you get ripped off this boat and have the life sucked out of you?"

I dropped the storm jib and grabbed my stomach, bending over in pain.

"Don't think about it. Tami—don't think about it. It's over. It's over now. You'll be okay. You'll make it. Richard's at peace."

"Richard's dead. I know he's dead. I'll never see him again."

"It was quick. Quick."

What did the stupid voice know? Now it didn't sound like Richard at all. Angrily, I questioned: "Quicker than what's going to happen to me?" Not expecting or wanting a reply, I grabbed the sail and dragged it to the bow, securing it under the spinnaker pole.

I went down into the aft-cabin to collect the blocks I had discovered under a bunk.

Back on the bow, I rested a minute and in my mind I recalled the dynamics of a rigged mainmast. There were the headstay and the backstay. They secured the mast straight up from the bow and stern directions. Then there were the shrouds. They ran from the masthead to the deck, on both the port and starboard sides of the boat. All this rigging, the stays and the shrouds, were to hold a mast upright and plumb. "Okay, that's right." I mumbled to my-

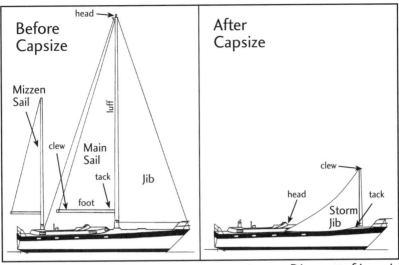

Diagram of jury rig

self, irritated that I had to concentrate so hard on what used to come so naturally.

I contemplated how the leading edge of a sail, the luff, in its normal position attaches to a tall mast. But my mast—the spinnaker pole—was short, a mere nine feet in the air. I decided I could use the shortest side of the sail, the foot, by setting the sail on its side and turning it completely over. The foot now became the luff, the side of the sail attached to the mast. The clew became the head where the halyard is secured. And the head became the clew where the sheets are attached. Then I could tie a line from the lower forward corner of the sail, the tack, through an eyebolt in the chain locker. That would allow me to adjust the tack at deck level and still leave enough length of sail for it to sweep the deck and collect as much wind as possible.

I went to work on my plan. I attached a line from the top of the pole to a fitting on the bow, and secured a second line from the top of the pole to an eye-ring back on the deck. This held the pole fore and aft. Next I rigged the shrouds, to keep the pole from falling sideways, by attaching shackles to the toerail on the starboard and port sides of the boat, and running lines through those to the top of the pole.

I pulled the storm jib out of its bag and rolled it out. I was afraid it would blow overboard even though there wasn't much wind, so I clipped it down and secured it as I went. I was now appreciating the effort Richard and I had spent in stowing this sail properly. I could easily find the three corners of the sail, the points of the sail I needed to rig, regardless of which side of the sail was up or down or sideways.

Getting the sail laid out, I ran a line from what would normally be the head of the sail, but which was now the clew, through the block to a winch in the cockpit. This would act as my mainsheet. I could sit in the cockpit and tighten or loosen the sail, depending on Mother Nature's whim and the amount of wind that matched her mood.

I rigged a block at the top of the spinnaker pole. I then ran a line through the block and attached one end to the head of the sail. The other end of the line I led to the anchor windlass. This created the halyard to my jury rig, allowing me to lower and raise the lopsided sail. I used the anchor windlass as my winch to keep the luff, or forward edge, of the sail taut.

I spent a whole day creating the rig and adjusting the lines that served as stays and shrouds. I then relocated the blocks and shackles in search of the proper angle that produced the most sail area. Finally, I hauled the sail up the pole and secured the halyard. I went back into the cockpit and adjusted the sheet. The sail was slow to fill, but she did. She carried only about thirty-six square feet of sail area, but that was thirty-six feet more than I had had two days before. I finally felt something different from pain. I felt hope. "We're flying, *Hazana*. Pushing two knots, I'd bet. Way to go, girl."

"Good job, Tami."

"Thank you, thank you, thank you," I said to the great emptiness. When the voice didn't respond, my enthusiasm faded. I needed that voice; it was becoming The Voice, the only thing for me to communicate with. It was more than me talking to myself, it was outside of me, yet in me. I needed The Voice's approval.

Even though there was no one to say, "Good job!" but The

Voice, I felt damn good about it. Even if the pace was only a knot or two an hour, it felt exhilarating. At least I was making way with some control of my direction. Besides, I knew if I didn't get home my mom would never, ever, stop looking for me. I was all she really had since my parents divorced when I was young—an infant. I feel like an infant again, I thought, I feel like Richard has just divorced me.

I thought about how my mother told me I could do anything— anything I had the guts to try. How's this Mom? Did you ever think I'd have the guts to try this? I pulled on the line tightening my newly created rig.

Taking a deep sigh, I looked at the compass and turned the wheel slightly to the three-hundred-degree course I hoped would get me to Hawaii. Then I bowed my head and cried, for I had no one, not a soul in this vast, watery, whole wide world, but me.

Chapter Seven

Time On My Hands

"Mayday. Mayday. Mayday. This is the sailing yacht *Hazana*. Isn't there one bloody person out there?" I said staring at the microphone in my hand.

The sound of static was maddening. I tried again: "Mayday. Mayday. Mayday. This is the sailing yacht *Hazana*. Does anybody hear me? Over."

The antenna had been attached to the top of the mainmast. With the mainmast gone there was no antenna. I could see the coaxial cable traveling overhead in the cabin to where the mainmast had been. I pulled out what was left of the severed cable and pushed it out the main hatch to one of the standing stanchions. Cutting the short antenna off the EPIRB, I taped its center wire to the raw end of the coaxial cable and then maydayed again but still heard only static.

To stay sane, I moved to the manual bilge pump for a while. About every hour I would send out a mayday, but there were so many hours of emptiness, of feeling lonely and scared, and as much as I wanted to I was unable to sleep. I sat at the wheel, steering, keeping *Hazana* on course. I thought and thought and thought. I thought again about my parents, my grandparents and my younger brother. How if I had followed in my mother's footsteps I'd already have a child in school and I wouldn't be in this mess. I'd be safe and sound at home.

"Yes, but you wouldn't have met Richard."

"I might still have met Richard. And he would still have loved me, even if I did have a child."

"But would you have taken your child out of school to go sailing?"

I could have home-schooled on the boat. Or, maybe my mom would have watched the child like my grandparents watched me.

"Do you think the child would have regretted you leaving?"

"No, why? I certainly didn't regret my mother having me live with my grandparents for a few years. They spoiled me. They absolutely loved me to death."

"What an odd phrase—'loved me to death.' Keep remembering how much they all love you, Tami, they love you to life."

"They love me to life." Well, they all certainly encouraged me to live my dream. Boy, if they could see me now. Some dream! A friggin' nightmare!"

My thoughts, as always, returned to Richard. We had had so many plans; how could it have ended like this? It just didn't make any sense. What about "God is good," and all that? What was good about this? Richard had been good. I'd been good. I just didn't get it. And there was no one to talk to, to help me understand. No one to share this grief with. No shoulder to cry on except the curve of Richard's guitar. I strummed the guitar lightly. At least it was a sound other than the waves slapping against the hull and the small shuffle of the awkwardly hoisted sail. I stared at the water and felt Richard all around me. If only he'd appear and hold me and make it all right as he had in the past.

I grabbed Richard's flowered shirt I so loved on him and squeezed it to my chest. As I rocked myself to sleep I thought of how I knew where Richard was; he was in my heart, but where was I? Perhaps tomorrow, at the blush of the morn, I'd find out. Day's first light has often revealed good boons.

The day broke clear and warm, with *Hazana* moving like a rocking horse in very slow motion. If the weather held, it would be a perfect day for my sun sights. The prospect of finding my latitudinal position in the Pacific gave me something to look forward to. It was a miracle the sextant hadn't broken in the capsize; it had been in its case, lashed down on a shelf at the nav station.

Taking the sun sight promised to be tricky: The capsize had ruined my stopwatch, and I didn't have a clue as to what had happened to my wristwatch. Only the clock in the main cabin, mounted on the bulkhead, remained to help complete the sun sight. The broken boom blocking the companionway would make it difficult. I was going to have to take my sight, carefully set the fragile sextant down, and then lean way over the boom into the companionway so that I could see the clock and note the exact time as precisely as possible.

When learning celestial navigation, I had had certain facts ingrained in me. I sat in the warm cockpit recalling the basics of celestial navigation and eagerly waited for noon.

I knew my chance of catching the sun at the exact second it reached its highest point in the sky, its zenith, was not that important, for the sun hangs at its zenith for about two minutes. It's fairly easy to predict these two minutes by going into the Navigation Tables and figuring out zenith-time mathematically. With the noon sight, I could try to identify where I was, at least know the latitude. My tentative plan was to reach the northern nineteenth latitude, turn left and hopefully reach Hawaii. The big island, Hawaii, stretches between latitude 19°N and 20°N, and being set to the north as I headed west should put me somewhere in the middle of the island, where Hilo is located. As noon approached, I became excited. I sat straddling the boom looking at the clock below, waiting for the second hand to hit noon. The minute it did I located the sun through the sextant and took my first reading. I carefully set the sextant down in its padded box and held onto the boom as I hung upside down to see the clock. 1201 hours.

Climbing off the boom, I repeated "1201, 1201" and went down below to the nav station. I opened the Nautical Almanac, the book that would give me all the information I needed to plot my position.

I methodically did my calculations. It was October 18, Day Six after the capsize. My sight gave me a latitude position of 18°N. This was astonishing news. I was much further north than

I had imagined. I glanced at the clock. There was no kink to its second hand, just its steady jump—one-thousand-one, one-thou-sand-two. But I was filled with doubt. What if the clock had stopped for a while and then started again? How could I be sure my latitude position was 18°N?

"If the clock is wrong, it'll screw everything up. If I'm too far south, I could miss all the Hawaiian islands and end up in China or some other far eastern port," I said out loud.

"Forget it, I'm just going to head for nineteen degrees north, hang a left and hope I don't miss Hawaii."

Anxiously I picked up the mike and maydayed again. Nothing. I glanced over at the galley sink; I was dying of thirst. I desperately wanted a drink of water, but I knew I had to ration. It was too soon to have more. But before I could stop myself, I jumped up and grabbed a cup, filled it with water from the hand pump and downed it.

"You're only stealing from yourself, girl."

Guilt-ridden I shouted, "I DON'T CARE. I HAD TO HAVE SOME." Throwing the cup down in the sink, I raced away from the nagging voice to the fresh air. The Voice didn't talk to me for the rest of Day Six.

Sitting at the wheel, the boat bobbing like a toy in a tub, nothing along the horizon, I let myself daydream. I remember how Richard and I always loved the idea of being the only boat in a bay. Like when we went to Fatu Hiva in the Marquesas . . .

Fatu Hiva has only two charted villages. Most sailors go into Hanavave, the Bay of Virgins, but Richard and I went into Omoa Bay because it would be more unique and less crowded. Huge stone pinnacles thrust up into the sky like sentinels guarding their village. With the anchor barely set and the sails stowed, we watched as an outrigger loaded with fresh fruit pulled up next to the boat.

"Bonjour. Ça va?"

"Pas mal. Et toi?" Richard cheerfully replied.

Mayaluga at anchor in Omoa Bay, Fatu Hiva, Marquesas

"Ça va, ça va! Je m´ appelle Jon. Et toi ?"

"Moi c´ est Richard, et ça c´ est mon amie, Tami."

While they carried on in French, of which I could only pick up bits and pieces, I studied Jon and his mild manner. He was slender, of medium height, with stomach muscles like a washboard. He had the local dark eyes, dark hair and dark skin. His face was extremely friendly and his smile bright.

Jon gave us a big sack of pamplemousse (grapefruit), oranges and papayas. He noticed our diminishing stock of bananas hanging from the boom crutch.

"What do you think, Tami?" Richard asked me. " Would you like to go to Jon's house later to meet his family and replenish our banana supply?"

"I'd love to."

Richard mapped out a plan to meet Jon later in the afternoon on the beach.

Even though I couldn't speak Marquesan and very little French, I had learned during my last voyage through the South Pacific that trading is big sport. There is definitely an art to it. An art of finesse. The locals are naturally generous, expecting nothing in return. The art is in learning to be naturally generous yourself, not appearing to trade because you feel you owe it, but rather because you love to give.

We had brought along trading stock: backpacks, flip-flops, thread in all colors, perfume, baseball caps, crayons, coloring books and baby clothes. A locker on board had been designated just for these goods. We loaded our backpacks with T-shirts, a baseball cap and perfume and went ashore. We had done a bit of trading on the other islands, mostly for fish, but also for the many acts of kindness our newfound Marquesan friends had shown us. We knew this would be another opportunity to give something back in return.

We rowed in early to explore the land and see the village. As we approached the beach, a swell threatened to swamp our dinghy. Richard back paddled, slowing us down. We rode in on top of the surge and hardly got wet as the wave diminished below us. We tied the dinghy up to a palm tree growing well above the tide line and walked up the beach to a grassy area where a couple of huts stood. They were somewhat like lean-tos with corrugated aluminum roofs. Several outriggers were in each of the huts. We found one outrigger prepared for a journey and walked up to it for a better look. The main body of the boat was made from skill-fully laid-up plywood. Two perpendicular wooden poles were

Friends next to their outrigger, Fatu Hiva

lashed to the canoe with rope. An outboard engine was attached to the stern pole, placing the steering handle next to the driver as he sat in the boat.

The outriggers were painted differently with bright primary colors. Streamline bird carvings adorned the bow and stern.

A man in his mid-twenties and a petite, shy, young woman walked up as we were admiring their boat. Through broken French and hand signals the man told us that he and his wife were headed to Hiva Oa for a supply run for the village. We helped them carry the boat down to the water's edge and watched as they rigged the outboard engine and expertly plow through the waves out to sea.

Just as the outrigger left, Jon came walking down to the water and greeted us. We followed him through the small village, passing houses and bungalows. The houses were made of cinder block or wood with corrugated aluminum roofs. Occasionally, you'd see a thatched roof. The yards around the houses were not manicured, just leveled brush cut back away from the home. Beyond these yards, the lush jungle prevailed with indescribable beauty. Everyone appeared to contribute to the self-sufficiency of the village. One family made bread; another raised chickens. One family built an addition onto their house and stocked it with the odd canned goods, shelf cheese and boxed milk—the local store.

Jon's front porch was cheerfully painted white and turquoise. A stream ran down alongside the house. Banana and fruit trees grew in abundance right in the front yard. We met Mareva, Jon's wife, and their two children: Taupiri, an five-year-old boy, and Lovinea, an infant girl. Mareva was a stunning, tall Marquesan woman in her late twenties. She had silky long black hair and arresting black eyes, a real beauty. Yet, when she smiled, sadness came over me. Many of her teeth were missing.

Mareva invited us into the house, and we sat down around the kitchen table. After we shooed the chickens off the table and moved the baskets of breadfruit and taro to one side, Jon joined us as Mareva served coffee in soup bowls with a spoon. "Taofe," Jon announced, pointing to the bowl of coffee. Sweetened condensed milk was passed around. We watched Jon to see how to drink our taofe. Jon generously poured the milk in until his taofe looked like melted vanilla ice cream. The islanders seemed to use the sweetened condensed milk everywhere—on bread, in their taofe and in their babies' bottles. Unfortunately, the locals' love of the sweet milk as well as sugar and fruit caused massive tooth decay as evidenced by their wide, gaping smiles. I never noticed a toothbrush or anyone brushing their teeth.

Mareva set a fresh baguette on the table. Jon tore off a hunk for himself, passing the rest to us. We watched him dunk his bread into the taofe and eat it, smiling and nodding encouragement to us. Jon would alternately pick up the bowl, sip the taofe, put the bowl down, and then dunk his bread in it just before he took another bite. We followed suit and enjoyed the first course of our humble meal. Mareva then cooked chicken in coconut cream, with baked taro, rice and boiled breadfruit. The chicken was moist with a hint of sweetness, but I didn't particularly like the boiled bread-fruit—too gooey.

Throughout the meal we talked in broken French and used hand signals to communicate. We learned Mareva was born on Fatu Hiva along with three brothers and two sisters. Her father, now deceased, was half-French and half-Polynesian. He and

Mareva and her children

Mareva's mother had built a colonial-type house to raise their family. Mareva asked us if we wanted to come the next day to see the house and to meet her mother and sister. We said we would be delighted, and that we would also like to purchase some tapas. Jon said he would take us to the tapa maker the next day.

We learned that Jon's family lived on Tahuata. Jon had met Mareva when he was visiting a friend in Fatu Hiva. They fell in love and were married. Their two lovely round-eyed children sat quietly at the table staring at us. Jon had built his own home and made his living fishing out of his outrigger. He explained that the island functioned mainly on a barter system. Everyone makes enough money to get supplies from Hiva Oa. The island exported copra (dried coconut meat), bananas, papaya, art work such as tapa, and wood carving.

For dessert, Mareva served us poi made from fermented breadfruit mixed with coconut cream and sugar. It was mushy, with the consistency of pudding. I liked it, but I noticed Richard ate very little.

We finished our meal and followed Jon out to the stream running alongside the house to wash our faces and hands. The wind was freshening, and I could see that Richard was getting concerned about *Mayaluga*. I decided this would be a good time to break out our trading stash. I reached inside my backpack and pulled out some baby clothes. When I handed them to Mareva, her eyes grew as big as saucers. She held them up and gave me her sparse-toothed grin. I had also brought a dress and perfume and thread, as well as a T-shirt for her son.

Next I pulled out a San Diego Padres baseball cap for Jon. He put it on right away. They were so appreciative of these inexpensive but desirable gifts; it was very touching.

Richard turned to me and said, "Jon is asking us if we'd like to have a 'lie-down' with the family."

"I know a rest is the custom after a large meal. Do you want to?" I questioned.

"Not really, I'm a bit worried about *Mayaluga*," Richard admitted.

Richard expressed our regrets to Jon, and we made arrangements to rendezvous the next day to buy tapa and meet Mareva's mother and sister. We bid them farewell with the customary cheek-kiss good-bye, and Richard saying, "Nous nous sommes bien amusés" (We've enjoyed ourselves).

When we got to the bay we were glad we hadn't had a lie-down. *Mayaluga* had dragged anchor toward shore. She drifted thirty yards before luckily the anchor caught again. We rowed out and reset the anchor, this time letting out more line. Once reanchored, Richard and I enjoyed our own version of a "lie-down".

━━◦⊂⧈⊃◦━━

The next morning we awoke early and went ashore. We were eager to go see the tapa man. Jon was ready and waiting outside on his porch as we came up the village path. We had come pre-pared since he had told us it would be a long hike. After walking along jungle paths for some time I heard drums beating. The rhythm loud, strong, consistent.

"Richard, what is it? The beating?" It unsettled me. Thoughts of wild, unfriendly natives jogged through my mind.

We were walking on a well-trodden track, beautiful, with dense lush ferns on either side. We came upon a smaller path where we turned and started to climb. The pulsing, hollow sound was get-ting louder with each step.

Richard asked Jon, "Qu´ est-ce que c´ est, ce fracas?" (What is that noise?).

"Tapa," Jon casually replied, tapa being the bark of the paper mulberry tree which is flattened into cloth and painted with geo-metric designs.

Jon was taking us to meet Henry, the tapa man. We came to a clearing and in front of us was what looked like a thatched tree house. But as we approached, I could see that one side of the floor rested on low pillars dug into the side of the hill, and that the other side was secured with two-by-fours to coconut trees. The walls of the house were made with palm fronds, and the roof was corrugated aluminum.

Below the tree house, in a level clearing, three women sat beating tree bark with short, baseball bat–like sticks against the trunk of a fallen coconut tree. We startled them, and they quit beating and smiled demurely. Jon approached and spoke to them in Marquesan. During his conversation he turned and pointed to us. We nodded and smiled. The oldest woman pointed to the thatched hut and nodded, and Jon waved at us to follow him up the path.

The front door was square and only about four feet high; we had to bend down to enter. Inside, the hut was dimly lit, even though two large glass windows were open. An old man in tattered shorts sat hunched, painting a tapa spread on a large table located in the corner of the twenty-by-twenty-foot hut. "Ia orana" (good day), said Jon, causing the old man to look up.

"Maeva" (Welcome), the frail grandfather said, as he got up and came over to Jon and kissed both his cheeks.

Jon introduced us to Henry, who kissed our cheeks too.

Henry's hunched back and weary eyes indicated he had led a strenuous life. He seemed glad to have company and bid us to come sit on a bench at the table for a cup of taofe. The steady sound of pounding resumed outside. The rich taofe was heavily laced with sweetened condensed milk. Henry rolled a cigarette, and he and Jon spoke nonstop as Richard and I looked on. I glanced around the house, noticing pots and pans and a couple of wooden chairs. In the corner on the floor sat a double-sized mattress covered with a tafaifai, a handmade two-layer Polynesian design patchwork quilt. I was intrigued by Henry's simple surroundings.

Jon would occasionally translate their conversation to Richard in French, who in turn would translate to me. The conversation evolved to our wanting to buy tapas. Henry became excited. He waved us over to his work table where a two-by-four-foot piece of tapa lay. I noticed this cloth was different from the supple cloth the Samoans and Tongans make for clothing. Henry's tapa was coarser and thicker, mostly used for painting and, at one time, storytelling. Henry had a mixture of tapas made from paper mulberry, breadfruit and banyan trees. The painting in progress was the familiar scene of a Marquesan warrior covered in many body paintings, but from the waist down to the feet was one big design of paisley print. Henry appeared to be half finished with the piece. His bowl of thick black ink was made from one of the local roots. He used a paint brush of human hair lashed onto a stick. The only thing not handmade was the thumb tacks used to hold the tapa flat on the table top.

From an old trunk, Henry brought out many tapas to select from. We chose five we liked. From our backpacks, we pulled out trading items. He wanted to trade a backpack and a pair of flip-flops. We finally convinced him to take some money as well.

We said good-bye to Henry and walked back down the path to where the women were methodically pounding out the cloth. The older woman was Henry's wife, Jon told us, and the two girls, his daughters. The girls kept looking at me and giggling. I smiled at them and asked Richard why he thought they were laughing— was it something I had done? Richard asked Jon and then explained to me that the youngest girl would like to touch my hair.

"Really?" I said surprised. "Sure." I motioned for her to come over.

The girl appeared to be in her mid-teens and so shy that she would hardly look me in the eye. I leaned my head over to make it easier for her to take hold of and rub my long blond hair between her fingers. She glanced at her sister with a smile. I motioned for the sister to come over too.

The sister promptly came over, gently rubbed my hair and said, "Nehenehe."

In French, Jon said, "La belle," to Richard.

"Yes, beautiful," repeated Richard, proudly looking into my eyes.

I smiled at him and then at the girls, thinking how odd it must be for the young Marquesans to see blond hair. Their own thick, black hair was also waist long, but tied back and much shinier than mine.

I reached into my backpack and pulled out some lipstick and perfume.

"Un pour vous, et un pour vous," I said to the girls. Before the sisters would take the gifts, their eyes pleaded with their mother. She nodded yes to them.

"Merci, Madame," each girl quietly said to me, switching to French.

"Il n´ y a pas de quoi" (It was nothing), I replied.

I smiled and stared at the women; thinking how exotic they looked in this remote and tropical setting. It was so peaceful and serene.

Focusing my eyes on the peaceful and serene sea brought me back to the dreadful situation. It was day six after the capsize. The sun was scorching hot and there was not a breath of wind. *Hazana* floundered and I floundered with her. Out of desperation I went below to straighten things up. Looking around the main cabin I didn't know where to begin. I carefully made my way to the V-berth thinking I should start forward and work my way aft. I couldn't believe how many things that belonged in the main cabin and galley were now scattered about in the V-berth. I know we capsized, but with this much damage and the way things are thrown about the cabin I knew we must have pitchpoled too.

I came across an oar. Perhaps I could use this to flag down a boat I thought, but how would it stand out? I glanced around and then remembered a red T-shirt of Richard's that said, Bay Scuba ~ Our business is going under, on it. I tied it around the oar's blade. Red, the color of love—the color of blood

"Red, the color of rescue," chimed in The Voice.

I tossed the oar up into the cockpit.

Making myself continue to clean, I tackled mopping the grunge out of the bilge since I had to step in parts of the bilge to get around the cabin. I filled a bucket with saltwater and found a sponge. As I mopped around a floor frame, something scraped against the ragged fiberglass hull. I pinched the object with the large sponge and pulled it out. My God, it was my wrist watch. How in the hell did it get in there? This was a God send. I dunked the watch in the bucket of saltwater and, with forefinger and sponge, rubbed the grunge off of it. Staring at it, I watched the seconds tick. 0933 hours I read on its face. I glanced at the clock on the bulkhead, noting its time of 0935 hours. Deeply cheered, I burst out loud, "Now I can do a morning and afternoon sight and really find out where I am." I dropped the sponge in the bucket, went over to the nav station and grabbed a pencil and paper. I took the sextant out of its box and tenderly carried these life-lines-to-land topside.

Straddling the boom I located the sun through the sextant. I slowly pulled the release on the sextant's arm, which lowered the sun down in the lens to the horizon. I pushed the lap-time button, starting the timer on the watch. Then I swung the sextant side-to-side just enough to get the bottom of the sun to skim the horizon line. When I observed the bottom of the sun tap the horizon line, I took a mark by stopping the watch. The recorded time read 0954 and 27 seconds. I looked where the arrow pointed on the arc of the sextant and wrote down the degrees. Then I did the whole procedure again, taking a total of three marks. These three marks would give me a choice of the reading I felt most accurately marked the moment the sun hit the horizon.

I took the watch, sextant and paperwork below and calculated with the Nautical Almanac and Sight Reduction Tables my LOP, line of position. With these numbers I plotted my LOP on the plotting sheet. "Well," I uttered to myself, "I'm somewhere on this line."

Near noon I eagerly did the whole thing over again. I was really excited because this sight would be "the fix," the sight that would tell me where I was.

I found myself to be on longitude 134°W by latitude 18°N. This was good news. I was closer to Hawaii than I had thought.

At 1400 I did my third sight of the day, but I couldn't get a good sight with the clouds shadowing the sun, so my afternoon fix barely counted.

I was eager for Day Seven to arrive so I could take my sights again and see how far I had gone during the night.

As the day opened very calm, I wasn't needed at the wheel. To keep my mind off Richard I went below and got back to my cleaning chores. Much to my joy I came across two sails, the mizzen staysail and the MPS, multi-purpose sail, which is a huge light-weight sail, somewhat like a spinnaker. Perfect! The mizzen staysail would be better in the light air than the storm jib I had raised. If only it fits the jury rig, I thought.

It was a challenge to push the mizzen staysail's dead weight out of the forehatch and get it to the foredeck. I had gone below to get more lines, when suddenly the boat heeled. Oh no, I thought and quickly scrambled topside to find the mizzen staysail over-board, slowly sinking into the sea.

"No, no, no. Damn it. Will I ever learn?" I ranted and raved. Then I sat down and cried.

"You have to stop crying, Tami."

"Shut up."

"You need that water; you're getting dehydrated."

"Just shut up. They're my tears. I'll cry if I want to!" I yelled.

But I knew The Voice was right. Crying would not help. I wiped the tears from my face with my fingers and licked the tiny drops. With a deep breath I stared at the storm jib hanging limp on the erect pole. What was the point? Maybe I should just roll off this boat like the mizzen staysail and be done with it.

"Maybe you should be happy you have the storm jib and get on with your first sight of the day."

"Shut up!"

I looked at my watch. It was almost 0900. I went below and got the pencil, paper and sextant.

My first sight looked good.

But my noon sight threw me. I calculated 132°W by 18°11"N. I had lost two degrees of longitude! Thats what? 120 miles. What happened? I wasn't as far west as I thought. This was becoming a horrible day. Everything was going wrong. I sat at the wheel fuming and angry. Disillusioned, my body and mind gave in to all the aches and pains.

At 0200 I did my third sight of the day. Yep, two degrees off. To ease my frustration I opened a can of sweet peaches, and spent hours nibbling on each slick, copper spear.

Chapter Eight
Water Above, Water Below

It was cold. I put on jeans and a foul weather jacket and went back to sitting at the wheel, steering like I had been doing for the past couple of days. I spent most of that time trying to remember why it had been so important for Richard to stay topside and not come below with me before the capsize. It was now Day Eleven. It had been an uneventful day. No ships. No one answering my maydays. Sporadically I'd maneuver the manual bilge pump and feel the pressure of water being sucked out of the bilge as I pulled the lever up, and then plunged into the sea as I forced the lever down. I pictured the grungy stream of water as it exploded out of its through-hull fitting into the vast sparkling sea. The mixed molecules and particles of pain, blood, food and debris, finally set free to dissipate into the now stabilized Pacific Ocean. How could I suck myself through the fitting and be set free?

It didn't dawn on me until the clouds were overhead to consider the old salt's saying: "Red sky in morning, sailor take warning."

As the first gust of wind slapped my cheek and the ominous black clouds spit rain in my face, I began to shake uncontrollably. A storm was about to break. Adrenaline pumped through me, fear squeezed from every pore, and I reacted in desperation. I buckled the EPIRB back on my waist, forgetting it didn't work, and strapped on my safety harness, clipping the tether to the binnacle. I examined the D-ring. It could part; Richard's had. What should I do? I wondered in panic, but I knew there was nothing I could do.

I eased the sheet on the jury-rigged sail. I thought of taking it down but I knew with this wind I could make some headway and every inch counted. I just hoped the jury-rig would hold. I felt as if the spray and rain were drowning me but the boat was riding well taking the seas on the starboard quarter. Was this the beginning of another hurricane? Without a radio I had no way of knowing what to expect. I felt uneasy in the growing swells.

"SHOULD I GO BELOW? SHOULD I GO BELOW?" I cried out to The Voice.

"Don't lose ground. Stay on course. Fight for your life," it ordered.

I leapt up and screamed at the clouds: "I'M NOT AFRAID OF YOU. YOU'RE NOTHING COMPARED TO HURRICANE RAYMOND. NOTHING. YOU'RE JUST A SQUALL. COME ON. COME ON, I'LL SHOW YOU. I'M ALIVE. ALIVE AND ALONE OUT HERE IN THE MIDDLE OF GOD-KNOWS-WHERE, SO COME ON, GET ME. I DARE YOU! COME AND GET ME! COME ON! TAKE ME TO RICHARD. I WANT RICHARD. RICHARD. I WANT RICH . . ."

I collapsed in the cockpit, wrapping my arms over my head to protect myself from the avalanche of rain and saltwater spray. I wept and finally begged.

"Please. Take me to Richard. I miss him so much. I can't stand this."

The driving rain on my back pounded the guilt deeper into my soul. I should not have left Richard alone topside. I should have stayed with him. He had needed me and I had let him down . . .

As exhaustion eased my intense guilt, I realized I should be collecting fresh water, but I just couldn't move, I was so distraught.

The squall dispersed as quickly as it hit. I was exhausted yet cleansed in a way. I hadn't realized how much I was still holding in. I was experiencing two facets of grief: grieving for Richard as well as feeling sorry for myself. Feeling sorry for myself was the easy one, the quieter one. The hollow hole in my heart for Richard, however, was terrifying. It exploded from me, and I had no control. I scared myself.

Times would be better, I told myself, when I reached latitude nineteen degrees north and could bare off to port and catch the trades for Hawaii. I sat and steered until late in the night, glad to be making way towards my goal.

The next day I had newfound strength. Maybe I'd simply had enough of feeling sorry for myself. I decided to check out the fresh-water tank mounted under the cabin sole. If I could get to an inspection plate I could unbolt, then I could lift it to see if any water was left. There was bound to be some. I found an inspection plate but one of the floor frames blocked access to it.

I searched through the scattered tools until I found a hammer and chisel, but the thought of chiseling through the wooden frame was daunting. Maybe there was another way. I grabbed a flashlight and started searching the top of the tank for another inspection plate. Most of the tank was situated under the saloon table and settee, making it hard to see, let alone reach. As I moved the beam of light around the fiberglass tank, I found another inspection plate, but it too was virtually impossible to get to without tearing the floor apart. Scanning the tank further, I found a loose wire with a connector on it dangling free. I moved the light across and saw the fitting on the tank. Excited, I extended my arm back into the narrow space, grabbed the loose wire and stretched it back to where I could push the connector and fitting together. Getting up, I stepped over to the galley and tried the pressurized faucet at the sink. Nothing but sputtering and spitting. As I started to return to the tank, I saw that the water gauge on the galley bulkhead now read a quarter full, and realized the fitting I had just reconnected was the gauge to measure the water level in the tank. I had a quarter of a tank of water! Overjoyed, I let it sputter and spit air out of the line and filled a plastic cup to the top and drank the most delicious drink I had ever had in my life: cool, clear sweet water. I filled the cup again. Oh, thank you, Lord, thank you.

Encouraged, I went topside and danced around like Rocky, sharing with the world my life-saving find: "WATER, WATER, EV-ERYWHERE, AND ALL THE WHILE DID SNEAK; WATER, WATER, EV-ERY WHERE, NOW THERE'S LOTS TO DRINK!"

Prancing some more, I hollered: "YOU CAN'T KILL ME NOW.

I'M GONNA LIVE, LIVE, LIVE. I HAVE WATER!" And with that I did every dance I had ever learned: the watusi, the jerk, the swim, winding down with a sexy bump and grind.

Laughing like a maniac, I hung onto the boom. Finding water was the most miraculous thing in the world to me. It left me giddy, even a bit hysterical. I had never been so thirsty as when I first realized I had to ration myself. Now, I no longer had to ration water, even though I would still have to be thrifty with the limited supply. Discovering the water was a great turning point. I knew I would live, but more so, I felt as if I wanted to live. A tremendous weight had been lifted.

That night I danced with Richard on the deck. I looked up at one of our favorite constellations, Cassiopeia, the queen. She is the big W in the midst of the Milky Way.

"Isn't she wondrous?" Richard had always mused.

"Wondrous like you." I'd whisper in his ear, knowing he'd reply, "Wonderful like you."

"Richard. . ." I called as I slowly waltzed about the deck, "The W is for water, love." Did God and the heavens know? Was it fate? Why didn't we know? Wondrous, wonderful, water. Did Cassiopeia know water would take you from me? Did she approve, encourage it? Did she want you? Couldn't she have given us more time? I put on Richard's shirt and hugged myself as I slowly danced. I closed my eyes. I didn't want to look at Cassiopeia anymore. I was jealous—Richard could be up there with her, waltzing along her wondrous path.

Chapter Nine

A Ship and a Gooseneck

Another long day. I tried to read a crinkily paperback thriller I had found in a cabinet, while I munched on a can of cold kidney beans. I couldn't focus that long on the book's small print; soon my eyes were blurry, and my head ached.

Half asleep, trying to stay on course on the windless day, I saw, as if in a dream, a ship, a big ship, smoke curling from its stack, a foamy wake trailing behind. "A FOAMY WAKE!" I jumped up out of my daze. A ship? "A SHIP!" I yelled.

I grabbed the flare gun out of the waterproof bag I kept in the cockpit.

BAM! The noise startled me. The flare shot toward heaven, its brightness competing with the sun.

BAM! I fired the second flare.

I stared at the ship. Nothing. It didn't even alter course.

BAM! went the third flare.

The ship was getting smaller.

I grabbed a smoke bomb and lit it with the waterproof matches in the flare bag. I was so nervous that when it stared to smoke I accidentally dropped it in the cockpit. I grabbed it to throw it overboard and burned my hand.

"GODDAMN IT!"

I grasped the oar with the red T-shirt tied onto it and rushed to the bow, frantically waving it as *Hazana* crested each swell. Nothing; the ship did not even alter course one measly degree.

Throwing the oar down I hurried below to the VHF.

"MAYDAY! MAYDAY! MAYDAY! DO YOU READ ME? OVER," I yelled into the microphone.

Nothing. Not one bloody blip.

"MAYDAY! MAYDAY! MAYDAY! DO YOU READ ME? OVER."
Nothing.

Dropping the mike, I hurried topside, grabbed the oar again and waved. The ship diminished quickly over the horizon.

I was shocked. How could they not see me? I'm right here. What was I supposed to do—jump in and swim to the damn ship? I stomped around the deck, kicking whatever got in my way.

"They should have someone on watch. What kind of stupid ship is it anyway? IDIOTS! YOU SHOULD BE DRY-DOCKED," I screamed at the ship. "MORON. I HOPE YOUR CREW MUTINIES!"

"AAAAAAAAAAAAAAAAAAH!" I screamed at the top of my lungs and then in frustration stuck my hand in my mouth and bit it.

"OUCH."

"Oh, that was smart," barked The Voice

"JUST SHUT UP, SHUT UP. I HATE YOU AND THIS FUCKING BOAT. I HATE EVERYTHING IN THIS WHOLE GODDAMN, FUCKING, WET WORLD."

Even with that tirade spent, I was still full of rage. With adrenaline pumping through my veins I paced back and forth on the foredeck. I kicked the four-foot section of the mainmast still attached to the boom. It was driving me crazy to have to continually crawl under the broken mast or go around to the port side and climb over the life raft that was still attached to the side deck. The foot of the mainmast no longer benefited *Hazana*, but getting rid of it entailed removing the clevis pin at the gooseneck

Starboard side deck. Note: Broken stanchions.

Mainmast binnacle ripped from the deck.

holding it to the boom. I stood on the foredeck and shrieked at the severed mainmast: "AND YOU. I HATE YOU TOO. I CAN'T EVEN GET TO THE BOW WITH YOU THERE."

I found the hammer and a screwdriver in the mess of tools in the aft-cabin. Sitting down on the deck, I beat on the stainless steel clevis pin. It didn't budge. I took out all my anger on that pin. Often I had to stop and rest. Finally, getting under the boom, I used my feet to lift the mast the fraction of an inch needed to relieve the pressure on the clevis pin. As the pin gave way and the foot of the mainmast slid from the boom, the mast fell on top of me, trapping me. Flat on my back near the toerail, I was terrified I'd fall overboard. As I tried to move, the jagged edges of the mainmast cut into my stomach. It weighed a ton. I didn't know what to do. I couldn't stay there; I had to get free. I was horrified I'd fall overboard as I lay gasping, staring at the sky, mustering every ounce of strength I could find to shove the massive piece of aluminum off me. As I lay there, I prayed: "Dear God, please help me. I'm sorry to be mad at you, I just don't understand all this. I'll try to be better. I'll . . . I'll—get this thing off me—one, two, three!" Arms pushed, feet shoved, stomach contracted and every muscle in my body strained to break free. As the chunk of aluminum rolled off me, I caught myself along the toerail, just before the momentum hurled me overboard.

I lay back against the warm deck, panting. How much more could I take? I should have realized the mast foot would fall on me. What's the matter with me? My sanity was treading water.

As my breathing slowed, I closed my eyes and Richard's image came to me. "Hi, Sunshine," he said in his tender way.

I reached up and caressed his cheek. He smiled at me. I put my hand around his neck and pulled him down to me. As I started to kiss him, I kissed my own hand instead. My eyes flew open; the nightmare returned. I lay sobbing. Could he feel how much I miss him? Couldn't he just come to me for one minute, one lousy minute? Hold me, dance with me, play—play boccie ball with me again, like we did in the Marquesas. . .

<hr>

When Jon, Richard and I reached the main road of the village in Fatu Hiva, we turned east and headed up the valley. After walking for about a half-mile, we came to the house Mareva's father had built. It was a colonial-style two-story, with a picket fence surrounding the front yard. It needed a coat of paint and some repair. What a contrast between this pillared colonial home and Mareva's single-story house, the more common style in the Marquesas. I pictured a French woman in Victorian clothing bursting out the front door and gliding down the front steps to meet her husband just home from the sea. Instead, through the front door came Mareva and her mother, Anna. They were both dressed in pareus of colorful cloth with bright red hibiscuses in their long, black hair. Would it be rude to pull the camera out of the backpack? It would have been a beautiful picture, but I left the camera in the pack.

Mareva and her mother came down the steps and greeted us with cheek-kisses, inviting us in. The house was light and airy— the windows open, the flower print curtains lightly billowing in the breeze. And although the fine antique furniture in the living room was limited, there was enough to make it stylish.

We were led into the kitchen where Mareva's sister, Hefy, was at the sink washing greens for the salad. A propane stove, sink and table were located in the inside kitchen and the outside kitchen area contained a large counter area, another sink and a cinder-block barbecue, where most of the cooking was done. Further out in the backyard was a pit called a himaa, or earth oven, where they buried and cooked pig. We knew it was a trained art to cook underground. Getting the temperature just right and relying on time, scent and intuition apparently were the keys.

When all the dirt and palm leaves were removed, we shared a bountiful feast of the most delicious roast pig imaginable. The unusually spiced meat was juicy, with edges of crisp, tasty fat. It was accompanied with taro, breadfruit, baked bananas, several types of squash, long green beans, manioc root (from which tapioca is made), salad with small tomatoes, and fresh baguettes. Poisson cru, a raw fish marinated in coconut cream, miraculously appeared. For dessert, we had the traditional poi and fresh fruits of all kinds. And, of course, there were bowls of taofe. What a feast!

The meal was served on large coconut palm fronds called niau, and we sat on woven pandana mats. We picked out what we wanted, setting it in front of us, using our fingers as utensils. People were coming out of the bush to join the tamaaraa. There must have been at least thirty people sitting down at one time. From noon to dusk, neighbors meandered by. Some would stay and eat; others just came to chat.

A game of boccie ball began. A small tag-ball made of wood, called the jack, was put out on flat ground. Each player had three boules (balls), about four and a half inches in diameter, to throw at the jack. The person whose boules came closest to the jack would win. Mostly men played the game, but occasionally women got involved. Richard and I joined in and played a couple of games. It took some time to get used to the weight of the boules, but the locals were tolerant of our lack of skill. Jon was especially good at the game. It was thrilling to watch him back up, his face a shadow of concentration, and then take off running to the throw line, heaving his boule as though he were a pitcher throwing a fast ball. When it landed it always knocked someone else's boule out of the way, and everyone would yell, "Une boule tirée! (One ball out)."

It wasn't long before I tired and let someone else take my place. I went to visit with Mareva and a group of women. My ability to communicate was limited, but we had fun talking in hand signals and teaching each other words, like tamarii, child in Tahitian, and potii, which means teenager. They thought it was very sad that Richard and I didn't have children, as kids are such a huge part of the island culture.

"We want to see the world—le monde—first, premier. En premier d´ abord, le monde," I said as I spun my forefinger in a circle. "D´ abord, le bateau," and I pointed to the boat and held up my finger as number one. "Then, le bébé," I said, pretending my stomach was swollen with child. They nodded, discussing it among one another, smiling knowingly at me. But I could tell there was no priority over children in their minds.

The women asked if I liked living on the boat. Most of them couldn't understand why I would want to live on the water. I pointed to my eyes and then spun my finger, saying, "I get to see le monde et vous"—I pointed to each of them. They liked that. "Vous," I pointed at them again, then pointed to myself, "get to see moi"— I patted my chest, and we all chuckled.

They wanted to know if I had brothers and sisters and if my parents liked the idea of my living on a boat.

"One brother," and I held my hand about two feet off the ground. "He's young, un bébé." And I shook my head, no, as to sisters, pointing to Mareva and Hefy. Again, they chatted among themselves. I got the impression they thought it was sad I came from such a small family. They asked about Richard's family, and I described that he, too, had only one sibling.

This relaxed atmosphere gave me the chance to study the faces of each woman sitting in the group. From the very old to the youngest, their faces showed the color and crevices of life in the sun. Their arms were muscular under the fat that came from their diet. Most of their day was spent planting and gathering food for meals, or washing and cleaning. They lacked the conveniences of the modern world that I took for granted. I knew they worked hard for what they had. The village worked as a team;

almost everything was traded, money meant very little.

As the afternoon gave way to dusk, I helped some of the women pick up what was left of the feast and fed it to the pigs and chickens. Even the eels in the stream ate the leftover fish. Every morsel of food perpetuated life. The few serving dishes were washed in the outside sink fed by running water from a gravity system that started at the nearby stream. There was no refrigeration. The simplicity was mind-boggling having come from America, where so many people think nothing of throwing a half of a sandwich in the trash.

When all was cleaned up, we bid everyone good night. Richard and I kissed many cheeks and thanked the family for the good time. Holding hands we walked back to the bay where our dinghy awaited. The night was calm and we felt very mellow and contemplative. How different this society was from ours, and how different this culture would be from the next. That's why we were traveling, to learn and be a part of the great big world out there.

Chapter Ten

La Cascade

After the horror of almost falling off *Hazana* and the joy of reliving the tamaaraa with Richard, I decided to trail a three-quarter-inch rope off the stern in case I fell in. Even with *Hazana* traveling only one or two knots I knew I might not have the strength to swim fast enough to catch up with her so, if I did fall in I could at least attempt to grab on to the rope. It terrorized me to think I could possibly drown after all these lonely and miserable days of struggling to survive.

Looking behind me, I could see the rope leaving the stern, but I couldn't see it tracking underwater. Nevertheless, it gave me a great sense of security to know it streamed about twenty-five feet behind *Hazana*.

Most days were about the same, sailing along at a snail's pace, but I did see progress each time I noted my LOP, line of position, on the chart, plus I had enough water and food to survive.

Sardines were my favorite meal. The flat, oval container was so distinctive that there was no mistaking the contents, even with the label washed off. I knew I shouldn't eat them—their salt content was way too high, making me thirsty after each delicious bite—but sometimes I just didn't care. I craved them. I'd hold out and hold out, and then finally when I couldn't take it anymore, I'd snap the can opener onto the rim, watch the oil ooze out, then crank the delicacy open. Using my fingers I'd dig in, grabbing a small slimy fish by its tail, and then nibble away. I'd spend an hour savoring half a can, saving the other half for later.

I stayed on a starboard tack, crawling to latitude 19°N. I was beginning to get apprehensive about seeking the higher latitude since there is sixty miles between each latitude the wind can be really variable. I seemed to be getting into more fluky wind, not as steady as it had been in the lower 18°N latitudes.

I went down to the nav station and grabbed a couple of books that hadn't been ruined in the capsize and brought them topside. I wanted to study the books in hope they would help me analyze my situation.

I decided to use the north equatorial current as much as I could to push me west. The current's force against the hull helped drag *Hazana* through the water, and I could make better time by using the current than by using the unsteady winds. The north equatorial current runs between latitudes 10°N and 20°N. Because I had found my watch and could calculate my longitudinal position, I decided it would be better to stay in the lower portion of the eighteenth latitude until I got closer to Hawaii; then I could climb northwest through the latitudes toward my destination. This, would also keep me in the path of more shipping lanes, where I hoped my flares would be seen.

As the night pushed away the day I made a pact with myself to try to stay awake longer into the night. My flares could be seen better at night if a ship were to appear.

Sitting under the star filled sky I reflected on how different the night sky is in the northern and southern latitudes. I thought I could see the Southern Cross but it was just a memory floating in my mind. It would be a long night, so I laid back and let my mind float. I floated back to La Cascade in Fatu Hiva . . .

The morning was beautiful, fresh from the rain during the night. The fragrant scent of the frangipani flower permeated the air. Richard and I sat in *Mayaluga*'s cockpit sipping cafe tres chaud, hot coffee, gearing ourselves up for the day-long hike to the grand waterfall.

We each stuffed a swimsuit, towel, water bottle, a couple of beers, and part of a lunch in our backpacks. Richard grabbed the machete. We were learning to carry it with us, for it was handy to whack open a coconut here and there and enjoy its refreshing milk. Rowing to shore we waved to a passing outrigger heading out to fish. Beaching the dinghy, we dragged it up to where the sand met the grass. Since we would be away most of the day, we knew it would be better to leave the dinghy up high and dry.

We walked up the path that led through the village and stopped in at Mareva and Jon's house to confirm our directions to the waterfall.

We found Mareva and her sister Hefy, at home playing with the baby. Hefy gave us explicit details of how to get there. We thanked her and kissed both ladies' cheeks and the baby's forehead good-bye and headed out.

After walking up the path through the rest of the village we came to the split in the path and took our first right. Things didn't look as I expected. I guess I envisioned a well-traveled trail and a forest ranger to appear in his Smoky The Bear hat to ensure us all was well. We could hardly tell that we were on a trail at all. Luckily we had the machete and could bushwhack until the trail reappeared. This went on for about two miles. I kept asking Richard, "Can you see another trail to the left?"

"I can't see a damn thing!" he would answer back.

We could tell we were gaining altitude when we finally came to a clearing and saw the magnificent vista. The day was warming up, and we were both sweating because of all the trail pruning. As we stopped for a rest, Richard looked over to me and said with a totally serious look on his face, "Hey, love, shinny up that nui over there and cut us a couple of jelly-bellys to suck down." It struck me so funny that I started laughing, hard. Me, shinny up a coconut tree! My laughter became infectious and soon Richard joined in.

Once we regained our senses we took a serious look at our location. In the distance we could see the meandering trail we still had to travel, curving its way in and out of the trees. As we followed it with our eyes, we saw it come out onto a sheer cliff about a 150 feet above the water. How on earth could we cross that spot? I contemplated turning back. Not wanting to sound like a wimp, I said to Richard, "Maybe that's a different trail."

Richard grinned and winked at me, and then took off up the hill. "Come on love, we have cliffs to conquer!"

Resigning myself to being a sport, I followed behind. The higher we climbed, the less vegetation we found and this made it easier to hike. But, as we tracked further inland, the vegetation thickened into a florid valley. Tiny waterfalls flowed down the lush mountainsides. Wild hibiscus, scarlet and crimson, flourished. We came upon a stand of banana trees and we each snapped a banana off, peeled back the skin and devoured the sweet, soft fruit. I was glad to take a break.

As we hiked out of a grove of uru, breadfruit trees, on the opposite side of the valley, we looked back at where we had trudged. The view was breathtaking. From where we stood, the foliage appeared a yellow-green velvet wrapping itself around the steep, dark lava cliffs. Tropic birds with long red tail feathers glided above the treetops. We could hear the rumble of cascading water churn and mesh with the ocean below. We stood there holding hands, absorbing this visual blessing. Richard put his arms tightly around me. Without saying a word, he gave me a loving, lascivious kiss, and then whispered, "Of all the people in the world, you are the only one I would want to spend this moment with." We looked into each other's eyes. I didn't need to respond, I just held him tight. He knew I felt exactly the same way.

Our moment of ecstasy was broken when out of nowhere two local men appeared. Each man had on a backpack with a rifle slung over his shoulder. They were dressed in earth-tones, not fatigues, but obviously trying to camouflage themselves. I was visibly startled. The man closest to us waved his hand and shook his head as if to say, don't be afraid. When his partner caught up, he said, "Bonjour."

"Bonjour," we replied simultaneously. Richard burst into French dialogue with them while I tried to compose myself. Richard turned to me and said they were goat hunters, but, sadly, returning home empty-handed. I felt relieved to know we weren't being ambushed, and Richard found out we were on the right trail and that the waterfall wasn't much further. The men left as quickly as they had come, and we charged on ahead with renewed commitment to reach our destination.

We hiked for about another hour. The trail was rocky and treacherous, with switchbacks that led up the side of the mountain, but finally leveled out and headed west to the sea. When we could see the surf below, I could tell we were getting close to the scary cliff we had seen from the other side. The path became very narrow and fell two hundred feet down to the surf pounding the rocks below. I couldn't look down. It made me dizzy. The trail had virtually disintegrated in this spot. We pondered the situation and decided if the "goat guys," as we had fondly named them, could do it, we could too. Richard went first. I stood by quietly saying a little prayer. There was only enough room for one foot to rest on the tiny ledge. Holding onto the rock outcropping with his left hand, Richard moved his left foot onto the ledge. His foot slipped, causing volcanic rock and dust to tumble into the surf below. I sucked in my breath. Richard's grip on the crevice and his right foot kept him grounded. With the heel of his left shoe he kicked at the narrow ledge making a better foothold. "Not to worry, love," he casually said to me. I watched him gauge his momentum and then swing his right leg around the sharp ridge, landing on solid ground. "Nothing to it." He beamed at me.

"I don't know about this," I murmured, not looking him in the eye.

"As you swing around, stretch out your hand, and I'll grab your wrist. I promise."

"I don't know . . ."

"Come on, love. We can't have come this bloody far to give up now."

"I hate heights," I whined.

"You go up the mast."

"That's different; I have safety lines holding me when I'm up there."

"It's not as bad as it looks," he said encouragingly.

"Okay, okay. Just be ready."

"I will, I promise."

I followed his foot pattern, and as I swung around he grabbed my wrist and pulled me right to land. "That, that wasn't so bad." I stuttered.

"That's my girl," he said, with a huge smile.

We continued over the trail, which had started to climb, and we took more breaks as we got winded. My calves and thighs ached. The steep grade took us up a ravine between two mountains and finally we reached a plateau and, violà! There stood a volcanic stone wall with a 3 1/2 foot-tall tiki, a human-like sculpture, carved into the stone. We knew tikis were used in the old days for religious rituals, and for sorcery, and guessed that this tiki was to protect La Cascade. It wouldn't be much further now. I followed Richard as he clambered over a large pile of rock. He arrived at the crest first, and I heard him whistle. "Tami, it's unbelievable! Quick, check it out."

When I reached him, he helped pull me up onto the large boulder he was standing on. As I turned my gaze in the direction of La Cascade, I was dumbfounded. The massive waterfall hissed and roared as it plunged into the reservoir, creating swirling pools

Tiki wall at La Cascade

of cloudy blue icing. Sparkling vapor rose and clung to the foliage, collecting the dew and dripping it back, reborn, into the natural pool. Pandanus, mimosa, paper mulberry, aito, haari, and nui trees covered with bromeliads rustled in the wind from the force of the falls. The fragrant frangipani, passion flowers and birds of paradise blazed in the tropical jungle and scented the air. Philodendron leaves were like hands waving in the great waterfall's breeze. Never had I seen such a mesmerizing sight.

In the calm area of the pond in front of us, something undulated. Could it be an underwater eddy, I wondered? A large flat rock in the middle of the pool basked in the sun.

We jumped down off the boulder and Richard took me by the hand as we walked around the perimeter of the pool to a level grassy area. A perfect picnic-site. Looking at the water I saw the undulation again. "Richard—eels," I squealed and turned in time to see him in the midst of a perfect dive into the crisp cobalt blue water. His pack and shorts lay piled up on the water's edge. The eels shimmery skin glistened in the sunshine. The idea of eels slinking against my body, scooting around my legs, nibbling on a toe . . . Yuck.

Richard surfaced with a loud Tarzan cry, pounding his muscular bronzed chest. "Come on in, love, the water's great."

"Richard, there's eels!"

"No big deal, love. They're more afraid of you than you are of them. Trust me, come on . . ."

"No way." I set my backpack down, getting out my towel.

Richard swam all over the pond, splashing and whooping it up. I sat on my towel in the sun and watched the water cascade off the high cliff.

Soon sweat was rolling down my armpits and cleavage. It was sweltering. The eels didn't seem to be bothering Richard. What the hell, I mumbled to myself. I pulled off my pareu, curled up like a cannon ball and jumped in. Surely my exploding into the water would scare away any lingering creatures.

The water felt cool, refreshing as it washed over my sunburned body. The water was so clean, thin, not dense like the salty sea. I surfaced, taking a deep breath. A sense of rejuvenation surged through me. I swam around stretching my arms out wide, freely kicking my legs. Floating, without a care in the world, I stared up at the sky framed by the lush foliage surrounding us. Ah, if this wasn't heaven, I didn't know what could be.

"Come on let's explore." We treaded through the water to get as close to the waterfall's intense shower as we could. Taking deep breaths we dove under the waterfall, where I tried to open my eyes but couldn't. We both surfaced, gasping for air.

"Look over here," said Richard as he guided me away from the mainstream of the falls to the smaller side falls. "Lets sit here for a minute and let the falling water massage us." We lounged under the descending water and let its fingers knead our hardened bodies. As my muscles relaxed, I heard Richard's voice echo out from behind one of the gentler falls. "You should see this, love." I waded over to him behind the pewter curtain. Richard sat a third out of the water on a rock. I leaned back and then let my feet float up, my toes popping out of the water. He took hold of my ankles and gently pulled me to him. Pulling my ankles apart he wrapped them around his waist, drawing my body tightly up to his. "You know waterfalls are a very manly thing," he said in a low voice, his sapphire eyes intently staring into mine.

"Oh yeah? Manly?"

"Yes. Manly," he smiled, "it's the way they come blasting over the mountain."

"Oh, I get it."

His left hand stroked the back of my head. He tenderly took hold of my hair and lifted it off my breasts letting it fall on my back. My body arched, aching to get closer, tighter to him.

"I feel like a wild man out here in the middle of nowhere. It makes me desperate for you—your love," and he lightly bit my upper lip then passionately kissed me. As our bodies united, our souls became one. We made love matching the intensity of the cascading waterfall, our cries muffled by the roar of the water.

We stayed in each other's arms for a long time while our pounding hearts quieted. Richard's stomach suddenly growled. We started laughing.

"Hungry, love?" I teased.

"I guess."

"Then I have a feast for you, my wild man. Take me to shore, and I'll serve you."

Richard scooped me up in his arms and plowed through the curtain of water. "I am a caveman bringing my woman home. You belong to me; you're mine, all mine." And he howled to the jungle.

"How did I get so lucky?" I pecked his lips and then pushed against his shoulders. He let me slip into the water.

"Last one to the food's a rotten egg!" I blurted out. Pushing off with my feet I swam like crazy toward the shore of our grassy beach. I hit my towel, panting. Richard grabbed me, I giggled, and he gave me a monstrous kiss. "God, how I love you," he whispered in my ear.

I laid out our feast: French bread, cheese, liver paté and papaya. "The beer's in the shade under that pandanus tree," I said, pointing to a spot in the water a few feet away. Richard stopped drying his golden hair and dropped the towel. I watched his striking body saunter to the water's edge. He stepped into the water and, sensing my look, turned and smiled the most loving smile at me as he raised his arms, flexing his biceps in a perfect muscle-man pose. I laughed out loud at his silliness, but deep down I thought he looked like an Adonis.

We sat in comfortable silence and ate, taking in all the divine wonder around us. This had to be heaven.

Feeling sleepy, we moved our towels over to a shady spot. I snuggled my back into the curve of Richard's body and fell asleep. The next thing I knew he was nibbling on my ear, whispering, "Sorry, love. It's time to go."

Reluctantly, I opened my eyes and stretched. "One last dunk, okay?"

Richard pulled me to my feet. "To the rock and back," he challenged wide-eyed. We both dove simultaneously into the enchanting pond, raced to the rock and swam back to shore. The placid center of the pond roiled from our race. Packing our belongings, we left the last of the bread for the black noddy birds watching us from the trees. "I will never forget this place," I said taking one last look as we headed out.

"Nor will I, love, nor will I."

The hike back to the village seemed less strenuous, probably because it was downhill, but also because we weren't in anticipation of what La marvelous Cascade would be like. We made good time returning to the village. Exhausted, we decided to head straight for *Mayaluga*. We would see Jon and his family tomorrow.

Carrying the dinghy down to the water, we rowed out to

Mayaluga as the sun set. As almost always, the sunset was gorgeous—awe-inspiring. The water looked like pounded copper. The warm breeze ruffled the palm leaves, playing peek-a-boo with the night's first stars. We saw a fire up the beach and watched some locals gathering wood.

We secured the dinghy and climbed on board *Mayaluga*. Richard clipped our wet towels on the lifelines with clothespins while I went below and cleared out our backpacks. I poured us a drink of sweetened lemon syrup, water and gin. We sat in the cockpit, facing shore, nursing the cocktail and feeling extremely content with our strenuous day.

The fire on the beach blazed now. We could hear guitars, tambourines and the clashing of sticks keeping time to the upbeat tune. The laughter and chatter increased, as more people arrived. Soon we could hear a lovely melodious Polynesian song begin. We felt as if we were being serenaded. What a perfect ending to a perfect day. We were both too gratified to move.

"See how proudly Leo sits in the sky?" Richard asked.

"Which constellation is Leo?" I yawned, teasing him.

"Right below the Big Dipper; he curves like a backwards question mark."

"Oh yeah. I see that old lion." Then I laughed at fooling him, for Leo was an old friend of mine.

"I feel like Leo tonight."

"King of the jungle, or a backwards question mark?"

Laughing, he said, "Definitely king of the jungle."

Centaurus—the centaur, half man, half horse—reared the upper half of his body in the sky. Richard pointed out that the two brightest stars of Centaurus are the pointers to the Crux, the Southern Cross. Centaurus is one of the biggest constellations and includes Alpha Centauri, the third brightest star in the sky.

"Did you know, love, that centaurs were considered monsters, yet they were capable of doing good deeds too?"

"No, I didn't know that," I stated nonchalantly.

"Oh, some of those centaurs could be outrageous, you know, get rip-roaring drunk at celebrations and break things to smithereens. But, thanks to Chiron, who is Centaurus, the Greek heroes were taught the art of both war and peace."

"It's pitiful to mature and realize war is an art," I said, shaking my head.

"There's an art to everything created on this earth, love. It's part of the synchronicity of things. Just look at that magnificent sky. It's a great big canvas of light. One constellation enhancing another, full of mythological stories. What stands out most to you?"

"The Southern Cross."

"Exactly. But, what does that simple cross up there mean to you?" he asked.

"I never really gave it much thought. I just know when I see it up there I'm in the Southern hemisphere. What does it mean to you?"

"It means I have traveled a long way from the different constellations of my childhood sky in England. It gives me enlightenment. See the direction the staff points?"

"Yes."

"It points to the south celestial pole. Too bad there's not a 'South Star' like there's a 'North Star'." Richard sighed deeply. "I do feel blessed with Crux up there shining down on us, but I feel more blessed with you here beside me. It's fate, Tami. I sailed half the world to find you."

Richard stretched his left hand out to me. I grasped it. It was warm and strong. I looked up at his angular profile and noticed the glint of a tear in his eye. I wanted to squeeze his hand, to bring that unconditional gaze of uninhibited love back to me, but I realized I had caught an unguarded glimpse of my lover's soul. He had returned his gaze to the sky and the privacy of his thoughts. It was not for me to invade. No other words or glances could have further authenticated our love for one another.

Our hands stayed grasped together in the center of the cockpit. I, too, returned to the theater in the sky, remembering something my mom used to say: "God's in his heaven; all's right with the world."

I felt this night would stay with me forever.

Richard let go of my hand and held his right hand up to the moon. "The old man's waxing," he said.

"How can you tell?" I questioned.

"See how my right hand caresses the right side, the full side, of the moon?"

I let go of his left hand and held up my right hand up to caress the moon. "Yes."

"That means he's waxing, getting full. If your left hand could circle the full side of the moon that would mean he's waning."

" I don't know about this."

"It's true. I learned it from an old salt in South Africa. By the look of this moon it should be full in less than a week. If we want to arrive in the Tuamotus on a full moon, we should probably leave here soon."

La cascade

Chapter Eleven
Hinanos and Cigars

I didn't care if the moon were waning or waxing when *Hazana* and I finally reached land. I just wished my landfall would be tomorrow. I was so tired of looking at nothing beyond the carpet of ocean and the curtain of sky.

My day-to-day schedule centered around my three daily sun sights. At night, if I had good wind, I'd steer *Hazana* as long as I could stay awake. Then I'd lash the wheel and sleep until the morning sun forced me, sweating profusely, from my sleeping bag.

My first chore upon rising was to look three hundred sixty degrees around the horizon. Nothing was there, ever, but water and sky.

My second chore took me forward to check the jury rig, to see if any lines were chafing. I made sure the luff of the sail was tight. The rig had become my companion, always there pulling the boat inch by inch toward the solid ground I longed for.

If there was no wind, I'd lash the wheel and force myself to go below to clean and dress my wounds. I didn't like this job, but when the bandage became oozy with blood, I had no choice; infection concerned me tremendously.

But down below debris still littered the bilge. The floorboards were askew, and I found it easier to move around by stepping on the floor frames and parts of the bilge than to try and figure out which floorboard went where. The scattered beans were sprouting and the oatmeal grew moldier by the day. Occasionally, a rusted can burst and started to stink, then I'd toss it overboard. It was just easier on my nostrils and nerves to stay topside.

Finally, the gnawing reality of living in a pigsty became too much. I couldn't take the filth and stench anymore, The Voice interceded: *"It's disgusting in here."*

"I know it."

"You need to continue the clean up."

"I don't feel like it; it makes me sick."

"It would make you less sick if you'd clean it up."

"You clean it up."

"It's your job."

"I'm in charge here—it's not my job!" I said cockily.

I stood a moment trying to decide who should win, The Voice or me.

Ultimately I realized it was a no-win situation. So, then the big decision became, should I wash the sprouting black beans off the bunks first, or attack the moldy rolled oats glued into the crevices of the woodwork?

"Don't be picky—it all needs to be cleaned!"

How could I argue with The Voice. It all did need to be cleaned. I got buckets of saltwater and started scrubbing. When I got tired of that, I'd start picking up cans of food and stockpiling them in the galley. Broken glass made me angry all over again. We should not have left so much glass on board.

As I cleaned, I came across three plastic bottles of hand and body lotion. This must be good stuff, I thought, for the owner, Christine, to have stored so many. Christine was a pretty woman. Ah, to feel pretty again.

I went to the mirror in the head and stared at myself. Even though tan, I looked pale. There were bags under my eyes, I was drawn, and my mouth had a perpetual pout. The bandage on my forehead was smudged with dirt and the paisley print bandanna crowned everything. What was I, I wondered, the Queen of Doom? I flipped the cap open and smelled the lotion. It smelled wonderful, the fragrance fresh and clean, citrus like with a hint of floral. I squirted some in the palm of my hand, and then rubbed it on my cheek. It felt cold, soothing. I rubbed my other cheek, then my eyelids, nose and chin. I stayed away from my wounded forehead.

I tried to smile at the mirror's reflection, but my lips were dry, cracked. I rubbed them hard with the lotion, trying to smooth away the crevices, but it didn't help much. I looked so weird, I scared myself. I didn't want to acknowledge the fears under the surface of the person I was looking at. It was a balancing act: I realized if I wavered too far I would go off the deep end.

I turned away from the sorry image in the mirror and made my way to the settee in the main salon where I sat down and proceeded to make trails of lotion along both arms. The cool sensation briefly raised goose bumps, but the satiny cream fed them and they disappeared as quickly as they rose. My skin sucked in the lotion. I spent a long time giving every pore on my body a taste. Between my toes, back of my neck, even my armpits. I couldn't get enough. When I finished I realized I had used practically the whole container.

Snapping the cap of the lotion shut, I looked around the cabin and thought, why even bother with this mess?

"Because it still stinks, remember. You haven't finished cleaning."

With a deep sigh, I lowered myself to my knees and reached deeper into the settee lockers. I felt something cold and pulled my hand away quickly. Grabbing the flashlight I shined it back toward the corner. Metal tins. I reached in and slid the containers out. Cigars! What on earth were cigars doing on board? I hadn't noticed Peter, the owner of *Hazana*, smoking them. Maybe they were for trading. I tore off the seal and lifted the lid of the tin. The aroma actually cheered me. In the past, cigarettes and cigars had disgusted me, but today they felt like a touch of humanity. The scent gave me a sense of being in a real world.

I dug deeper into the settee and pulled out a big tin of Arnott's biscuits. "Ummm." I surprised myself. My appetite must be returning. I tore off the lid and ate one, savoring each crunchy bite.

"What else is hiding in this gold mine?" Turning sideways I reached way in. My fingertips scraped a cardboard box. Stretching with all my might my fingers hooked and dragged the box to the opening of the settee. Ripping it open, I discovered a case of Hinano beer—Richard's and my favorite.

"Man, I could get wasted on this," I announced to no one. "I bet if I drank it all, I could die of alcohol poisoning."

"What would be the point?"

"The point would be to quit remembering the good times I will never have again."

"Do you wish you had never had those good times?"

"I wouldn't give them up for anything."

"Then enjoy remembering them."

Sometimes I hated The Voice. It slapped me with logic every chance it got. No sympathy for my plight. Grabbing a bottle of beer, a cigar and the bottle opener and some waterproof matches out of the galley, I went topside. There was no wind; the sun was setting. Straddling the boom, I bit the end off the cigar just as I'd seen in movies and spit it overboard. I stuck the cigar in my mouth, biting it with my front teeth and struck a match to its tip. Sucking and coughing, I finally got the stogie lit. I snapped the bottle cap off the Hinano and watched it sail through the air. Even though the beer was warm, it tasted like nectar. Feeling like King Tut on his throne, I lounged there contemplating the passing of another day.

Could that bright star near the horizon, the one with the red hue, be Fomalhaut, the eye of Piscis Austrinus, the southern fish? I knew Fomalhaut was one of the four royal stars of ancient astrology. I could see no other bright stars near it—must be Fomalhaut. Later, I would look for the water carrier, Aquarius, and find the jar he carries and spills down onto the southern fish. As the last bit of light seeped from the sky, the winged horse, Pegasus, galloped into view—Pegasus from the blood of snaked-haired Medusa. As the myth goes, Perseus killed Medusa in one of his heroic deeds. Studying the sky further, I found Grus, the crane, and Lacerta, the lizard. If I looked hard enough, would I find Richard, the missing man? I pictured Richard's lovely face inside the great square of Pegasus. If only we could be straddling the boom together, smoking cigars and drinking warm Hinano beer. If only . . .

I heard the foot of the sail scrape taut along the port side of the deck. Ah, some wind. I finished my beer and snubbed out my cigar and then climbed down from the boom, unlashed the wheel and started steering. At least at night I had the stars to entertain me, the moon to get lost in and no fear of running into anything. But I'd rather run into something, something alive and human that could save me, I thought. These nights were so different from our nights on *Mayaluga*, going into the Tuamotus, where coral reefs sprung from nowhere . . .

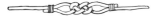

The atoll Raroia, in the Tuamotu Archipelago, was my and Richard's destination, five hundred miles away from Fatu Hiva. We settled into our at-sea routine of three-hour watches. We each did a daily set of sun sights: morning, noon and night. Then we compared our results. Richard had more experience than I did and turned out to be consistently more accurate. But I was usually close and learned quickly.

Our trusty wind vane, "Bucko," handled the steering for us. It was considered our second mate since it was so reliable when the wind blew. However, it was the watchperson's job to check the compass periodically and make sure we remained on course.

We made good time on our passage. We estimated we would be near Raroia around 0200 on the fourth day. Night is not a good time to be coming into the numerous atolls of the Tuamotus. Having sailed through them before with "good old Fred," I knew how tricky their few entrances could be, full moon or not.

We hove-to around midnight. Lashing the tiller, backwinding the staysail and reefing the main allowed *Mayaluga* to drift without making headway. The clear starry night and full moon added a mystical quality to the vast open sea. We made our bed in the cockpit by stuffing a couple of extra sails in the foot well and putting the cockpit cushions on top of them. We carried sheets and blankets topside and made a cozy nest. We brought up the battery-operated alarm clock and set it to wake the watchperson every half-hour.

I took the first three hour watch at 0000 hrs. Every half hour the alarm beeped, and I'd do a visual on the horizon. Always it was a boundless rolling sea. The wind picked up toward the end of my watch. At 0300 Richard took over.

I had been sound asleep, but suddenly I woke with a start. Glancing to my left, I noticed Richard peacefully sleeping beside me. I leaned up, grabbed hold of *Mayaluga*'s dodger and pulled myself to my feet to look around the horizon. Not five hundred feet from our starboard bow, waves were breaking and the swaying palm trees were backlit by the moon.

"RICHARD," I yelled, feeling my eyes pop out of my head, "GET UP, START THE ENGINE—WE'RE TOO CLOSE!"

He sprang to his feet in one fluid motion, throwing bedding, cushions and bags of sails out of the way to get to the engine controls buried beneath them. I quickly eased the staysail sheet and rushed back to the tiller to release the line holding it. With all the bedding in the way I couldn't reach the jam cleat holding the line lashed to the tiller. Knowing exactly where my knife lay in the cockpit, I grabbed it and cut the line free.

With the tiller freed and the engine roaring, we tacked and raced away from the atoll. We were both in shock from the close call. Adrenaline surged through me, and my heart beat louder than our engine. I asked Richard if he could hear it. He said not over the din of his own.

What was it that woke me, I wondered? We must have misjudged the speed of the current. I gave thanks to the heavens above that we hadn't gone aground.

Hazana sat as still as a lily pad in a pond. I hoped I had not misjudged the current. I prayed to God the speed of the current would propel me faster to the reefs of Hawaii. The crescent moon shown as a bright comma in the sky. I felt like an abandoned maiden. The night drifted on.

Chapter Twelve
Machetes and Eels

Sometime before dawn, a cloud the shape of a maple leaf fanned the slivered moon. I strained my eyes, but I was still at sea, *Hazana* was still mastless, and Richard was still gone.

Coming topside from calculating my morning sight, I found a booby bird sitting on top of the jury-rigged mast. It appeared to be about thirty inches tall and mainly white. I was fascinated with its beady eyes and powder-blue eye shadow. The feathers around its beak were also a pretty blue hue. Its huge webbed feet were a powder blue too and seemed out of proportion to its body. The bird left, but a couple of hours later came back to use the rig again for its resting post. It squawked and slept a lot and then, after preening itself, flew away to fish once more. The booby stayed for three days, but when its droppings started to stink, I tried to shoo it away with the red T-shirt–covered oar. The damn bird kept coming back again and again, and I kept chasing it, apologizing, and saying if it wouldn't poop it could stay. Finally it had had enough of me and flew away for good.

October 31, Halloween. With a steady wind, I had traversed forty miles according to the noon fix. I thought about all my Halloweens as a kid, the getting dressed up, the trick or treating with my friends. I remembered the year I got so sick. I was seven years old, and my grandparents had rented a flapper costume for me. I loved it because the fringe sewn on the satin material shimmied and the beaded head band glowed with fake gemstones. At the third house I trick or treated, I got very ill. I was devastated to have to go home: my bag of candy had only three pieces in it, and no one else would get to see me in my wonderful costume. I wondered what my little brother would be this year, probably a pirate or a cowboy.

That night on *Hazana* I decided to make myself a treat to take the edge off this trick I was living in. I opened a canned ham and poured plum sauce over it. I relished it with peanut butter and crackers. For dessert I delighted over each bite of canned pears.

November 1, twenty days after the capsize, I lackadaisically scanned the horizon with the binoculars as I did thirty to a hundred times a day. Suddenly I spotted something orange on the horizon. It was a large tangerine buoy with a red flag tied alongside it. I could see the bright buoy only as it crested the swells.

"Wow, will you look at that," I said to the cleat that held Richard's empty tether.

I altered course and about two hours later got close enough to the buoy to see there was a net attached to it. Should I tie up to the net and wait for the fish boat to return? What if it never returned? I wasn't sure what to do.

As I collected myself and studied the net again, I realized it must have been abandoned. It was too covered with barnacles, and fouled with streeling seaweed to have been set recently. No one was coming back for this net. I should sail on. I had already wasted two hours of precious time.

I made sixty miles the next day, and fifty the day after that. I was obviously in the north equatorial current. I was pleased I had listened to my intuition and stayed in the lower 18°N latitudes. I estimated only 590 miles to go to reach Hawaii. Only! Here I'd crawled at a snail's pace, almost a thousand miles of the Pacific Ocean all alone, and I was thinking "only." Land was near, yet still so very, very far.

For the next two days, it was rainy and the seas were rough.

A gust of wind woke me at four in the morning. I got up, unlashed the wheel and began to steer. The sail billowed out, full of wind. The rush of two knots through the water felt exhilarating as I sat propped up by some pillows against the cockpit coaming. I liked steering with my foot, my toes wrapped around a cool stainless steel spoke. My mind buzzed with alertness after hours of sleep. So, as always, I'd think. I'd think and think and think.

I wondered, why is there life anyway? Are there other civilizations in space? How are earth, water, sky, stars, people, animals all connected? Are we connected? I had felt connected to Minka, the German shepherd I had growing up. She could read my mind: She always knew when I was sad or melancholy, not quite up to par. I wished she was sitting beside me, her soft, furry head in my lap. I remembered how often Richard and I would have the same thought, mental telepathy. Could he and I still think the same things? Could he feel how much I miss him? If only Richard could be handing me the binoculars again and asking me to find the entrance to the atoll Raroia . . .

The shoreline of the atoll could have been an illusion as the morning light poured out the new day. But it wasn't. Richard and I were excited about visiting the Tuamotu Archipelago, the largest group of atolls in the world. An atoll, basically a barrier coral reef, in either a horseshoe or circular shape, shelters a lagoon that can be miles wide, creating a wonderful marine land to explore. The high points of the atoll, the land above water, called motus, are slender, sandy islets. Forty-seven of the Tuamotu atolls have no entrance, twenty-one have only one entrance, and ten have two.

I had climbed the mast steps to the first set of spreaders, and after peering along the rugged coastline for three hours, I finally spotted the concealed entrance to Raroia, on the west side of the atoll.

Sailing directions for the South Pacific warned boaters that the current could rip through the sixty-foot-wide entrance to Raroia at eight knots. We waited for the end of the tide's ebb; it was just about slack before we ventured in. We took down all the sails and carefully motored through the pass into the lagoon. Aloft, I kept my eyes peeled for those sharp coral heads just below the water's surface. Richard kept his eye on me as I pointed in the direction he should steer to avoid a collision. We crept forward, slowly. It was nerve-racking, but finally we made it in without a bump to our precious keel.

We anchored in a sandy bottom in front of a small village. While stowing gear from our four-day journey, we watched a twenty-foot runabout motor out to us from the shore. The hull was painted a canary yellow, and as it got closer I saw the deck was a bright marigold orange. Two men were on board, one in a white hat, shirt and shorts, the other in a green plaid short-sleeved shirt and red shorts. The one in white waved as they came closer. We waved back. He was obviously the official. The driver skillfully pulled up next to *Mayaluga* and turned off his engine. Richard and the official spoke in French. Richard turned to me and told me they had come out to invite us to their village.

The man in white, George, was the local gendarme and asked if our passports had been stamped yet anywhere in French Polynesia. Richard told him we had checked into the Marquesas. The skipper of the boat, Remy, was an extremely handsome man, in a rugged sort of way. I couldn't help but think how Hollywood would have loved him. He invited us to come and share lunch with his family. Richard accepted the invitation and arranged a time to go ashore later that day, after we had a chance to stow some gear on *Mayaluga*.

After the two men left, we made *Mayaluga* shipshape. We lowered the dinghy into the water and since it was still early in the day we went below for a nap before our lunch date.

A tap ,tap, tap, against the hull woke us. Richard jumped out of bed to see who it was.

"Tami, that was Remy. We're late for lunch." Still half asleep we both rushed to get dressed. As I stepped in the dingy with its bow line, Richard set the oars and away we went, rapidly rowing to shore.

The beach was of crystal white sand. Three local men sat under a coconut tree, in homemade driftwood chairs. When asked where Remy lived, they pointed to a lime green, single-story waterfront cottage that stood less than a football field away.

Remy came out to greet us as we walked up and introduced us to his wife, Lucy, their daughter, Sylvia, and Sylvia's fiancé, Kimo. We were made comfortable outside in chairs on the sand and enjoyed the smell of fresh tuna being barbecued. Sylvia came out with a couple of coconuts, nonchalantly whacked their tops off and handed them to us. As we drank from them we chatted as best we could in a combination of French and hand signals.

Lucy, straddling a board that had a metal grate attached, grated coconut as we talked. Sylvia would put handfuls of the grated coconut in a cloth and then twist the cloth to wring the cream out of the coconut into a bowl. She did this with all the grated coconut and then mixed flour and salt into the coconut cream. Lucy shaped the mixture into balls and dropped them into boiling water to make faraoa, bread.

The meal included crisp greens from the garden behind the house. It was delicious, as most home-cooked meals are when you've been out to sea. Taofe was served afterwards and never tasted better.

Sitting there, content, enjoying the beautiful view over the huge lagoon, I suddenly noticed a black-tipped dorsal fin. As I sat up and stared, I counted four more black-tipped dorsal fins. "What are those?" I asked, pointing.

"It looks like sharks," Richard said. Turning to Remy he asked, "Requin?"

"Oui."

"Merde!" Richard said.

"Oui, merde." Remy laughed, shrugged his shoulders and spoke rapidly to Richard in French. Richard then explained to me that the black-tip and white-tip reef sharks are not "mauvais," bad, like the great white shark, which Remy described as "effrayant et laid" (terrifying and ugly). The locals were terrified of the great whites because they have been known to cruise inside the lagoons and attack people.

"Are the locals frightened of these reef sharks?" I asked and Richard translated.

After a pause Remy rattled off something to Richard, and Richard translated for me: "The locals leave the reef sharks alone as they are only curious about people and not eager to eat them. But Remy said he wouldn't try to pet one." Richard laughed. "Remy also warned us to keep a dinghy nearby while swimming in the lagoon for a quick high and dry surface to exit the water."

Richard asked Remy permission to walk around the village. Remy exclaimed, "Oui, oui," and encouraged us to go explore. We invited the four of them out to *Mayaluga* the next afternoon. Remy explained they would be harvesting copra at another motu in the atoll the next day. Coconut trees, which live over sixty years, produce fifty nuts a year, he explained to us, and the oldest coconuts are cracked open and laid in the sun for the meat to dry. Once dried, Remy said, the copra would be bagged and collected by the copra boat, and taken to the mill at the inter-island wharf in Papeete. There, it would be processed into coconut oil used in making margarine, soaps, cosmetics, vegetable oil and candles for export.

We thanked them for the wonderful lunch and invited Remy and his family for a tour of *Mayaluga*. He said they could come out to the boat after work the next day as they would very much like to see her.

The village was quaint and adorned with a variety of broadleaf trees. We walked on a path that took us through the middle of the motu to the ocean side. There was such a distinct difference between the lagoon side of the motu and the ocean side: The lagoon was a peaceful turquoise lake, calm and inviting; the ocean side churned with pounding waves and frosty whitecaps.

Remy and his family motored up to *Mayaluga* the next afternoon. Apparently a yacht hadn't anchored in Raroia in a couple of years, and Remy's family was very curious to see the inside of *Mayaluga*. Once the tour was over, we sat in the cockpit. Seeing our guitars, Remy asked if he and Lucy could play them.

"Oui, oui. Je vous en prie," Richard said brightly.

Remy and Lucy both strummed a little and then flowed into a soft melody. Soon Remy began singing a lovely Polynesian song. We were enchanted, as well as surprised at the depth of their musical talent. Contentedly, Kimo, Sylvia and the two of us sat listening.

Later, we asked if we could visit some of the other motus of their atoll. Richard was curious as to how safe it would be for us to sail through the lagoon.

Remy and Kimo explained we could easily cruise around the lagoon, as long as we watched out for the coral heads, which would appear as a darker color under the surface of the aquamarine water. Kimo said we would be able to detect the coral heads more easily if one of us was up on the mast as the higher angle would cut down on the blinding refraction of the sun.

"Hey, Tami," Richard called down to me in the galley. "Remy said they don't harvest copra tomorrow, on Sunday, and they would love to take us to Kon Tiki Island across the lagoon after church. What do you think?"

"Would it be an overnighter?" I asked coming back up on deck with a bowl of popcorn.

"Yes. He said they'd camp on shore. We'd tow their runabout behind *Mayaluga* because they will need to come home early on Tuesday."

"It sounds great." I smiled at the faces watching me.

We made plans to leave the next day. Lucy mentioned we would be welcome at the church if we cared to attend. It started at ten.

The next morning we got dressed up. That meant Richard put on long pants and a flowered shirt with his flip-flops. I always wore a skirt in the villages anyway, but this day I picked one of my finer ones.

Raroia is primarily Catholic. The priest was a local man and the mass was conducted in the Tuamotuan dialect. It was surprisingly short yet very dynamic. A robust woman played the piano and belted out songs that brought tears to my eyes. The whole congregation sang while clapping their hands and swaying to and fro to the lively beat. The energy was dynamic, very inspiring. It wasn't like any church we had ever attended, which is probably why we enjoyed every minute of it.

Remy and his family came out to *Mayaluga* a couple of hours after church. We took off across the lagoon. Neither Remy or Kimo had sailed before so we taught them how to raise the sails and bring them in. The women were content to sit in the cockpit and watch, holding on and laughing as *Mayaluga* heeled in the wind.

The steady southeast tradewind felt wonderful blowing over our skin, and the reefs around the atoll, in-between the motus, protected the lagoon, creating a calm, flat sea and sailing "par excellence."

We arrived at Kon Tiki Island in early afternoon, and dropped the anchor in crystal clear water. Richard and I felt in awe of being at the motu where the famous balsa raft *Kon-Tiki* had run aground in 1947 after sailing from Peru in one hundred and one days.

We pulled Remy's runabout up to *Mayaluga*, and the family of four climbed into it and took off for shore. We lowered our dinghy in the water and soon followed behind. They were bustling about setting up camp when we arrived. We were surprised at how well organized they were. Obviously this was nothing new to them. Pots, bowls and blankets came out of their runabout. Kimo carried a five-gallon jury-jug of water to the camp, then dug out

Kon-Tiki Island, Raroia Tuomotus

tiny hooks and fishing line from the runabout. As Kimo started walking up the beach, he turned and waved for Richard to follow. Richard yelled back to me that he would be helping Kimo search for hermit crabs to use as bait .

With a small shovel, Remy dug a pit for cooking. The women and I collected palm fronds for bedding and coconuts for milk and meat. Lucy had brought the grater and settled into grating the coconut meat. I rowed back to *Mayaluga* and retrieved some flour and breadfruit I had leftover from the Marquesas.

By the time I got back to the beach, Lucy and Sylvia were cooking a bunch of small fish Richard and Kimo had caught. The barbecued fish smelled great. Our late lunch turned into a feast. I was beginning to think every meal was a feast.

Later, Richard rowed out to *Mayaluga* and brought back our guitars. He played solo for a while and then Remy picked up my guitar and joined in. The rest of us were lulled to sleep with their harmonious strumming and humming. The day was warm, the food excellent and now the soft harmony left me feeling totally at peace.

After the nap, Sylvia and I went looking for shells. I squatted at the water's edge and searched for the incredibly ornate shells hidden in the coral grit. Digging through the grains of coral I discovered a beautiful spiked shell the size of my fist. I became so intent on my unusual discovery that I fell backwards in surprise when I glanced up and saw black, beady eyes staring at me. Two black-tipped sharks were only two feet away from me. Taking a deep breath, I realized they weren't going to leap out of the water and eat me, but it was unnerving to know they had so silently intruded. They appeared only to be curious, but I didn't shell so close to the water after that!

That night we sat around the fire. Remy polished some handmade mother-of-pearl lures by using large fish scales that were slightly abrasive, somewhat like fine grit sandpaper. The lures gleamed from his effort. We took turns playing and singing our American and English songs for their Polynesian ones.

Lucy, Sylvia and I tired first, so Richard rowed me out to *Mayaluga* and then eagerly went back to hunt for lobsters on the reef with Remy and Kimo.

When Richard finally came back to *Mayaluga*, he was concerned about Kimo for he had lost his vision and Richard and Remy had had to guide him back to the camp. The family knew it was some type of fish poisoning and that it would need to work its way through his system.

The next morning Lucy boiled the lobsters for breakfast. What a treat, lobster for breakfast! Kimo was better, some of his vision had returned. After eating and cleaning up, we decided to go back over to the reef. Kimo stayed behind to rest.

We walked from our motu across the reef to another motu. The tide action felt good on my ankles, and I tended to lag behind, forever the sheller. All of a sudden, there was a frenzy of splashing in front of me and in an instant of fluid motion, Lucy swung her machete around and whacked the head off a moray eel.

"My God," I said, stunned. Lucy continued on, unfazed. I watched the body of the eel squirm and twist to its death. Now I knew why they always carried machetes. I stopped shelling and hung close to Lucy's side. I felt a new respect for her.

When we came back to camp, Kimo was much improved and wanted to go snorkeling with us. We all piled into the runabout and motored over to a large coral head we could explore. Underwater, the coral and its spaghetti tendrils appeared to wave to us but the coral was actually rigid, stretching for the sun.

The fish life around the coral head was mesmerizing: the indigo-and lemon-shaded angelfish, the spotfin butterfly fish with its dark line through the eye and near the tail, and the pumpkin and gold rainbow parrotfish with its beak-like mouth. When we spotted a couple of large turtles, Kimo and Remy swam like crazy trying to catch one, but with no luck. With all the mysterious beauty around me it wasn't long before I forgot about the black-tipped sharks.

Looking for Polynesian black pearls, Remy and Kimo dove for nakas, the giant black-lipped oysters. On the beach, Kimo cleaned the meat out of the shells and showed us their beautiful mother-of-pearl insides. The raw oyster meat was firm and much chewier than that of oysters from the colder waters of the Pacific northwest. Kimo showed us a couple of nakas that had the beginnings of black pearls inside them. He told us of the pearl farm on the atoll of Makemo, and said it and the small village was worth seeing.

Remy and his family were gone the next morning when Richard and I finally got up. We knew they had to leave early to get to work, but we never even heard their motor. Richard and I spent the next few days exploring other motus around the atoll.

The morning we were leaving Raroia, we sailed back into the village and anchored. Remy motored out and we told him we had to be moving on. He said he'd give us a ride to shore to say good-bye to Lucy.

Lucy shyly gave us a beautiful large turtle shell as a parting gift, and Remy gave Richard a three pronged spear he had made. They promised to say good-bye to Sylvia and Kimo for us as they were out cutting copra.

"Merci, Lucy. Ia orana (Thank you, Lucy. May you prosper.)." I said with tears in my eyes.

"Maururu roa, hoa (Thank you very much, friend.)." Lucy whispered back.

Richard kissed Lucy's cheeks, and we went back to *Mayaluga* in Remy's runabout.

At *Mayaluga*, Richard asked Remy to wait a minute. He dug around in his fishing box and gathered a variety of manufactured fishing gear he thought Remy and Kimo would like. Remy seemed pleased with the present. I quickly dug through our diminishing stash of gifts, hoping I still had a pair of thicker-soled flip-flops that would fit Lucy. Yes, I found the perfect pair with a maroon-colored strap.

Tears streamed down my face as I kissed Remy's cheeks good-bye. Remy was the most dynamic Polynesian we had met so far, a unique character. Richard gave him a hearty handshake that fell into a deep hug. A special bond had grown between the three of us.

The good-bye left me melancholy. We went about stowing the dinghy back on the foredeck. I was forced to recover from my woes when Richard suggested I recheck the galley to be sure everything was stowed before we galloped across the pass. After all, we were leaving almost two hours later than we had planned. That can wreak havoc when you miss the slack tide and have to deal with the ebb.

As I feared, the current was ripping and raging through the pass as we approached. I hung tightly to a stanchion as the madly ebbing tide grabbed hold of *Mayaluga*. This was not a ride I would care to take too often, I thought to myself, as the tide spit us out of the lagoon.

Chapter Thirteen

Overboard

My foot slipped off *Hazana*'s wheel and hit the cockpit sole with a loud thud. I looked around for the tortoise shell, Lucy, Richard and Remy. It was only another dream.

Lifting my foot back up on the spoke and giving a little push to port I thought of Richard going overboard and what a waste it was of human life. The Voice interrupted my thoughts: *"The only waste is your feeling sorry for yourself. You have no right to judge that Richard's life was a waste. You are not God."*

I felt ashamed, but then became defensive: "Hey, Voice, no problem, I'll never fall in love again."

"Now, that would be a waste."

I smiled at The Voice's wit and turned the wheel. Once again I noticed a stiff jerkiness in the helms's action. I could not keep ignoring the fact that something was damaged or fouled under the boat. I had inspected the wheel and steering cable topside a couple of times, but nothing seemed askew. I knew I had to check the rudder, and the only way to do that was by jumping in the water, diving under the boat and taking a look. The thought scared me. Who would pull me back on board if something went wrong? What if a shark got me? I didn't want to think about it anymore. I'd deal with it later.

The sky twinkled an unreadable Morse code. The stars were sending messages of encouragement my way. A shooting star meant I could have a wish. My wishes were always the same: Someone please find me; let Richard be alive; give me courage to dive under the boat. I loved this time of day, the edge of dawn. It seemed magical to watch the stars go to sleep one by one as the sun woke up.

This day, the sunrise painted the sky with Maxfield Parrish hues. I could feel serenity. Was God serenity? I lashed the wheel and went to the bow.

Unwrapping my flowered pareu, I let it slip to the deck, where I sat down on it, cross-legged, nude. I rested my arms on my legs, palms up, ready to receive all the good vibrations the universe would give me. Rays of pastel colors permeated my hair, my eyes, my skin, my forearms, my legs, my air and my soul. I took in a deep cleansing breath through my nostrils, more air and more air, then let it out through my mouth with a "whooo." I could feel the marrow in my bones warming in the morning's placid heat. I melted into harmony with all that was around me, and all the spirituality melted into me. At least for this brief time, I loathed nothing nor longed for anything. I felt no fear and experienced no pain. The bliss of the pastel morning had its own melodious song, its own gospel, its own amazing grace.

My meditation gave me strength. Optimism engulfed me with an innate knowledge that what is meant to be—is. Richard's time was up. There was maybe one chance in a million he could still be alive. Even if he had come below with me, it might have still been fatal. Perhaps God gave me a break. What if I had regained consciousness and Richard had been lying there dead? Wouldn't that have been worse? Yes, it would have been. And probably worse for him too; not quick, like the power of the monstrous wave that must have knocked the last breath out of him.

I wondered what makes it a person's time? Does God decide? Do our actions on earth decide? I've been a good person. I don't consciously try to hurt people. I don't lie or steal. I believe I need to treat people the way I want to be treated. We are all equal, no exceptions. But Richard was a good person, too. So, why am I still alive? Why wasn't it my time also? What am I living for? What will I do now with the rest of my life?

The tears that rolled down my face and dripped onto my breasts were cleansing tears. They were mourning tears and recovery tears cascading into one. The questions I asked myself were therapeutic. Every second of every day was therapy and a step toward recovery; I was achingly accepting my circumstances and slowly starting to heal.

I was sure the Bible said something about many mansions in the Father's house. Does that mean we live again, I wondered? To me it did. I wanted Richard to be reborn, to live again. I wanted to know him again, to talk to him again, to love him again. And maybe that's why I was meant to live, so I'd get to know and love him in a different way the next time. All I could do would be to live on and find out. Someday it would be my time, but not yet, and that was the hardest guilt to get over.

With a deep breath and a stronger whooooshing of my breath out, I opened my eyes and peered into the light of the sun. Its intensity blinded me, humbled me. Once again, I bowed my head to the great Creator and simply said, "Amen."

Opening my eyes I peered into the deep turquoise sea. It appeared calm, gentle. It beckoned me. Yes, I could dive under the boat today. With renewed energy and faith, I got up and stretched. Grabbing my cheerful pareu I went to the cockpit and dug around, stacking up two ropes and my dive mask. Should I eat first?

"No, dive first; then give yourself a treat."

"Fruit cocktail?"

"Ummm, yes. It sounds delicious."

I took off my bandanna and laid it on the seat locker. I briefly touched my hair—no—I did not need to think about my tangled hair. It would only force me backwards emotionally. Start with diving under the boat, I told myself.

I grabbed the two ropes and tied them onto the winch with a couple of half hitches. Then I tied each rope around my waist with a bowline. I still had the three-quarter-inch line trailing in the water off the stern.

As I stood on the side of the deck, I asked God to protect me. Then I took a deep breath and jumped in feet first. The water felt chilly but surprisingly refreshing. The saltwater burned my cuts, my head especially. But I didn't mind—it was healing. I couldn't remember the last decent shower I had taken. Since the capsize, I had either poured a bucket of saltwater over me or wiped myself down with a washcloth dampened with fresh water, but now, being totally submerged in the saltwater, every pore on my body was cleansed. I treaded water, allowing myself to get acclimated, and then put my mask on. I tried not to think about this being the same cruel water that had taken Richard from me. I took a deep breath and dove under the boat. The water was clear and refreshing. Seven mahi-mahi hovered against the hull. The bottom of the boat looked ominous with its large keel and small rudder. I surfaced for another breath as I tried to keep my anxiety and fear at bay.

Diving deeper, I swam toward the propeller. I could see that one of the mizzen shrouds had gotten wrapped around the propeller's shaft. After going up for air again, I dove back under and tried pulling on the shroud, but it had welded itself onto the shaft. It was easy to figure out that there was nothing I could do. There was no way I could hold my breath long enough to try to cut the shroud free, nor would I have the strength. Surfacing, I grabbed one of the ropes to help pull me nearer to the boat. My arms ached as I pulled myself up the ladder bolted onto *Hazana*'s stern. I shook my head in disappointment remembering how strong I used to be. Oh well, stiff steering is better than no steering. I was just thankful the rudder was in its place so I could steer at all. Feeling proud of myself for jumping in the water and overcoming my fear, I finished patting dry and went below to retrieve a can of fruit cocktail. I had to open three cans to find the one filled with fruit cocktail. Sitting in the cockpit, letting my snarled hair dry, I delighted in each bite of the treat. Every time I came to a halved red cherry, I set it aside, creating a small mountain of crimson sugar to devour as one great big bite.

"May I have one?" The Voice meekly asked.

I stared at my growing mound of cherries and thought, what the hell. "Sure—help yourself," I said, then chuckled, because it was The Voice that needed my help for a change. This felt good.

OVERBOARD

Chapter Fourteen
Turtle Back Sunsets

I took off my hat and lifted my face to the sun. A shadow crossed over my closed eyelids. Shading my eyes from the glare, I looked up at the sky. A pair of frigate birds were soaring in the wind. This was Day Twenty-six after the capsize. I had just taken my noon sight and calculated 480 miles to go. Seeing the birds felt like a good sign to me—land must be near.

Frigates have a huge wing span, six feet across. They dive, and at the last minute, tucking those giant wings against their body, they hit the sea like a bullet, resurfacing more times than not with a fish.

I couldn't bring myself to catch fish to eat. I would have to kill them. Death had taken on a new meaning for me now. Canned sardines were just fine. They were already dead, the life knocked out of them.

I spent many hours watching the frigates. Sometimes I'd follow their motions with the binoculars. It made me dizzy. The female was larger and aggressive, and easily stole food from the male. I decided he let her have it, for they must be lovers; he wanted to share.

When a different bird flew into view, I sat up and grabbed *Hazana*'s binoculars. It was a tropicbird, simple looking, about the size of a gull with a long white tail. It would have nothing to do with the frigates—most birds won't because the frigates are so big. This sighting was reassuring as it was a definite sign that I must be approaching Hawaii.

Life would have been much more boring if it hadn't been for the birds. But more important, was the fact they were a definite indication I was nearing land. In celebration, I dug out a can of sardines. I was sick of cold chili, cold beans and cold canned vegetables. I loved sardines. If the birds could eat what they loved, why couldn't I?

Five days passed uneventfully. I established a routine of waking up sometime between three and six in the morning, depending on the wind and swells. I'd check the rig, meditate on the bow, open a can and eat whatever was in it. It was always a surprise since the labels had fallen off most of the can goods. I'd try to pick a can I thought was fruit for breakfast. Then I'd scan the horizon with the binoculars, and sit and steer for hours and hours. I still couldn't read. I couldn't concentrate on words.

Noon was the most exciting time of day because I would take my second sun sight and calculate how far I had traveled in the past twenty-four hours. It was always somewhere between twenty and sixty nautical miles. I just prayed I would hit one of the Hawaiian Islands and not sail past them. It didn't have to be the big island of Hawaii I came to, even though that would be the closest. Any island would do.

I constantly thought about my past with Richard and what my future would be now that he was gone. My grandpa would encourage me to go to college. Philosophy? Why would I want to go to school and philosophize about life? All I'd been doing for the past month was philosophizing? I had decided human nature was unpredictable: If someone had warned me that I'd be in this situation and asked me how I'd respond, my answer would have been wrong. I wouldn't have had a clue without living it.

Maybe I could take sociology, I thought. After all, I'd witnessed firsthand several native societies the past few years. Or, how about Domestic Science? Gees, half the world was starving and the other half preferred to eat with their fingers, not concerning themselves with which fork to use for the salad. Besides, what good was knowing how to make a crème brulée, when a poisson cru was simple, tasty, and better for you?

Maybe psychology would be the major for me. I could study how the will to live is greater than the will to die—fascinating. No, no, college was not for me. I didn't know what I'd do. Anyway, now was not the time for making decisions about the future. Now was the time to persevere through each minute, and concentrate on surviving.

I never let myself drink a beer before sundown. Sometimes the sea melted into a sheet of glass at dusk. I'd crawl up on the boom, light a cigar and pop open a Hinano. This was usually the loneliest time of day. How many sunsets had I enjoyed with Richard? We used to play a word game: describing the sunset in exact colors. Words like violet, cream and chartreuse were easy, common. Richard would describe a sunset as perhaps, "flax with a hint of mandarin, blended with carnelian and absinthe." I would giggle, watching him cop an attitude as he pronounced his witty description. My best had been, "The vermilionette sun dispersed its petal-pink hues to primrose, parrot green and plum over the wispy garnet clouds."

"Bravo," Richard had laughed and applauded me.

How could I not ache with loneliness when the sky was once again flax with hints of mandarin and my Richard wasn't there anymore?

Sometimes during those lonely sunsets I'd talk to Richard, dare him to come to me. Other times I'd sing stupid songs. Songs with silly lyrics that repeated themselves ninety-nine times. I tried to sing upbeat songs, not songs with lyrics of home and love.

Back at the wheel, I adjusted my pillows and steered with my foot. I searched the sky for my constellation friends. As I crossed each degree of northern latitude, I'd discovered new constellations. I was pretty sure the hero, Perseus, was taking his stand in the sky now amid the Milky Way. Perseus holds Medusa's head in his left hand and his shield in his right. Perseus's goal is to rescue Andromeda, using Cetus, the sea beast's help. I couldn't help but wish that Richard were Perseus and his goal were to rescue me.

When I couldn't keep my eyes open any longer, I lashed the

wheel and crawled into the sleeping bag, hugging Richard's flowered shirt. Often I'd hold it up to my nose and take in deep breaths, reliving his scent. I could picture his loving face in my mind, and I'd whisper sweet nothings to the soft cotton. He'd whisper back how much he loved and missed me. In the first light of dawn I would still be hugging the shirt. Oh, how I loved that shirt, its teals and turquoises reminding me of the teal seas of the atolls. I remembered what a difficult time Richard and I had had finding the entrance to Taenga, as we sliced through the teal sea on a perfect beam reach. Wouldn't I now love to have the tradewinds filling the genoa and mainsail, heeling me over a comfortable twelve degrees. If only Richard could somehow be that one in a million and make it out alive.

Mayaluga heeled on a perfect beam reach from Raroia to the atoll of Taenga. After four hours I peered through the binoculars, searching for the entrance to Taenga. All I could see were giant waves crashing along reefs the length of the motu. We sailed parallel to the motu well offshore and then came about and sailed back. Sailing the length of the atoll again, we turned around, knowing an entrance was eluding us.

Finally I made out a concrete pad on the motu in the channel, on the opposite side of the breakers. Straining my eyes, I saw a few single-story buildings and a couple of bright splashes of color that must be local homes. Most atoll villages are established somewhere inside the lagoon, but this one, Taenga, was located along its entrance.

On our third pass, a local man zoomed out in an aluminum runabout. As he approached I could see he was bare-chested with shoulder-length hair. He circled, waving for us to follow him. We would have preferred to wait for the slack tide or even the ebb, but we didn't want to miss the chance of following this good Samaritan. As we motored toward the vaporizing white water, I felt very apprehensive. "Richard, I don't know about this."

"Tami, the bloke wouldn't be waving us in if we couldn't make it. Buck up, love. It won't be as bad as it looks." So I bucked up, and we motored in on the shoulder of the tubular six-to-eight-foot breakers that threatened to gobble up *Mayaluga*.

Wharf at Taenga

As we came around the line of swells, I could see the channel. It had been hidden between the breakers. Our escort made an up-and-down chopping motion with his hand, his forefinger pointing straight ahead. He obviously meant for us to stay in the center of the channel. I nodded a big yes. Richard pushed the accelerator forward, forcing the engine to full throttle. It was the only way to make it through the boiling five-knot current coming straight at us, a current that had the power to turn us 180 degrees in a heartbeat and drag us back out.

I kept my eyes focused on our guide. Never had I experienced such a precarious entrance.

Once inside the channel away from the gnarly breakers, we throttled back, made ready docking lines and fenders, and crept up to the concrete dock. A couple of locals eagerly helped us tie up. The good Samaritan took off inside the lagoon; we never got the chance to thank him.

"Je m´ appelle Richard, et elle s´ appelle Tami," Richard said to the two men.

"Je m´ appelle Meteta," said the man who was about the same age as Richard.

"William," murmured the younger, shy man.

We stayed at the dock for the rest of the afternoon. People came from all around, curious about the popaas, the foreigners, and their sailboat. We invited them on board to see *Mayaluga*, but soon too many people had accepted the invitation; our waterline was well under water.

One man appeared to be the leader of the village. We asked him in French for permission to walk the village and to sail to the other motus of the lagoon. He was pleased we had asked permission and graciously gave it. Seeing we were eager to go ashore, he shooed the people off the boat and then disembarked with us. He pointed to the path and waved us on to explore. We thanked him and eagerly went trekking through the small village. We didn't have to give our precious possessions on *Mayaluga* a second thought, as theft is unthinkable in the Tuamotus. There would be horrendous shame to the village and the family should a local steal anything, let alone something off a visiting yacht.

The village was immaculate. The walkways, meticulously lined with crushed coral and rocks, wound attractively around the village proper, veering off to the various homes. At the residences, the paths narrowed but continued in their tidy and defined way up to uneven wooden stairs and listing porches.

We came to a small white building with a cross on top of its steeple. I knew from my reading that the original Polynesian religion had died out in the early nineteenth century after the first missionaries arrived. Protestant missionaries had come to Tahiti forty-seven years before the Mormons and thirty-nine years be-

Exploring the reef at Taenga

fore the Catholics. On some atolls Richard and I had found two or three churches of these faiths, making for very intimate congregations among the small populations. Occasionally

Coral heads at sunset

an atoll sheltered only one religion, like on Taenga, where Mormonism prevailed.

As we sailed away from the dock, we adjusted the sails for the close haul into the lagoon, heading to the windward side of the atoll.

About halfway across the lagoon we reached a huge coral head standing well above the surface of the water. We took all sail down and let the boat drift while we snorkeled in the aquamarine water around the magnificent coral head. Its porous surface snapped, crackled and popped with life as reef and sergeant-major fish darted about. We watched a two-foot rainbow parrotfish—one of the largest coral-eating herbivores—make the rounds. Thick-lipped bluehead wrasses were everywhere. But my favorite fish at the coral head was the pearly razor fish—I liked the contrast of its milky light-fuchsia color sparkling in the turquoise sea.

As I gently kicked my long, wide fins, I thought about what an ancient species fish are—close to a half-billion years—the oldest major group of vertebrates in existence today. I felt privileged to be serenely floating on my stomach on the surface of a lake-like sea, the sun warming my back as I observed the alien world of the underwater.

Refreshed from our swim, we hoisted the sails again and headed for a motu whose outline looked like a turtle's back. I climbed the mast steps to the first set of spreaders and watched for submerged coral heads as we moved into shallower water. We dropped sail, set the anchor and had a cold beer with a bag of chips and a homemade salsa I had been saving. Such a life . . .

We stayed at "Turtle Back" a couple of days. I spent hours and hours collecting shells along the lagoon side of the motu. Richard windsurfed, and we snorkeled a couple of times a day, always with the dinghy at our side. The temperature of the water could lull you to sleep; it was so warm and comfortable. Most of the time we didn't even put on our bathing suits. It was as if we were the only people on earth.

Each day we walked across the motu to explore the fantastic barrier reefs on the ocean side. We carried our machetes along the cavernous sienna reef keeping an eye out for eels as we strolled sometimes in ankle-deep water, along the prickly curved slabs of petrified coral.

White water from breaking waves came rushing across the coral and crawled up our boots, then slurped away from us, back out to sea, only to return. As the tide receded we could hear air being sucked down holes in the hollow areas of the reef; within a few seconds the vapors would explode in the air with huge fountains of saltwater. Such magnificent blowholes.

Coral heads loomed out of the reef like giant sculptures. Each evening the sunset backlit these heads, creating mysterious silhouettes against the firelit sky. Amber, carnelian color blazed across the horizon. We sat as totems, wrapped up in the awe of the magnificent sky, worshipping the gift of another day well spent.

We left Turtle Back in time to catch the slack tide. The idea of going back out the ferocious narrow channel made me anxious. As we approached the entrance to the pass, we bounced over a coral head—bump-bump-bump—only a knick, thank God. At slack tide the channel was much tamer than it had been coming in on the ebb, and the swell action outside the pass had subsided as well. It would be smooth sailing for the five hours to Makemo, and according to sailing directions, the entrance to Makemo was easy compared to those of most atolls.

As we approached Makemo another yacht was just leaving— Americans, symbolized by the flag they flew off their stern. We waved to each other as two ships passing in the daylight.

Local kids swimming out to Mayaluga

We anchored in the lagoon near the village. It wasn't long before we heard children shouting and splashing their way out to *Mayaluga*. As they reached the boat we looked down on twenty smiling faces—ranging in age from five to twelve—treading water around us. We invited them all on board, and they didn't hesitate to climb swiftly up the swim ladder. There was not an ounce of shyness in the bunch. They ran around the deck chattering enthusiastically. I showed them the interior of *Mayaluga* in groups of three and four. Our pahi, our boat, was our fare, our house, I told them. They were so curious I had to stop them from opening lockers and getting into things. When we were ready to go ashore, the kids jumped off the boat and swam to land, racing us as Richard pretended to row harder and harder to beat them. They won.

With help from our little friends, we pulled the dinghy up on the beach and tied it to a nui.

"Où se trouve l´ élerage d´ huîtres perliéres?" Richard asked the kids.

One of the older ones volunteered to take us to the pearl farm, so we followed him along a sandy path. As we walked we admired the quaint multicolored fares along the way with bright Tahitian flowered curtains hanging in the windows. The flora surrounding the homes was just as brilliant, especially the hibiscus blossoms. Makemo appeared to be more lush with plants and blossoms than the other atolls we had visited.

The pearl farm lab wasn't far. It was a one-story building with

Friends house at Makemo

a concrete-slab dock on pilings. We walked in and noticed a small Asian man in a white lab-coat peering through a magnifying glass into a giant naka, black-lip oyster. In each hand he had a long, thin utensil with a small scoop on the end. With one utensil he would scoop up what looked like sand, and with the other scoop up a gooey, clear activator. Placing the two in the naka apparently started the precious Polynesian black pearl. The scientist intent on his job, never even looked up at us. Another man came in and collected the primed mother-of-pearl shells. He was taking them to the shells' nesting ground somewhere in the lagoon.

We spent one clear and balmy night at Makemo. Sitting in the cockpit that evening, I felt peaceful and content. The sky glittered with stars surrounding the more-than-half-lit moon. Holding my right hand up to the moon, I aimed to caress the old man's illustrious right cheek. Ah yes, a waxing moon when the full side fits in my right palm.

"Do you think a month will be enough time for us in Tahiti?"

"I don't know; I've been thinking about that too," Richard admitted.

"Bastille Day is only twenty days away."

"I'd hate to miss those canoe races along the waterfront. Do you think the quay will get crowded?"

"Yes."

"You do?"

"Every sailor in the vicinity goes to the Bastille Day festival," I said.

Richard held his right hand up to the moon. "He'll be full within the week. Maybe we should leave for Papeete tomorrow."

"Are you ready for the big city?" I teased.

"I'm ready for a good steak and kidney pie."

"I don't know if you'll find the two together in Papeete."

"But surely I can find all the ingredients and make one myself."

"I'm sure you can. In fact, I think you're going to be able to find more things than you ever imagined in Papeete," I said laughing.

"Good. Then shall we leave on the morrow?"

"The morrow it is."

Chapter Fifteen

In Broad Daylight

Day thirty-four after the capsize, with an estimated 240 miles to go, I was savoring my last can of sardines when—just like that—a ship came out of nowhere. Throwing down the can of sardines, I jumped up to get to the flares. I was so frantic, I tripped in the cockpit and fell, almost breaking my leg. I hobbled over to the watertight container in which the flare gun and flares were stored and tearing off the lid, I took hold of the loaded gun, held it in the air and shot. *BAM!*

"I'm home! I'm almost home. Oh, God, what will I say? I wonder if they're American?" I babbled as I loaded another flare and shot it off.

"Hold it girly—girl. You're not home yet."

BAM! Went another flare. "Oh yes I am. There! See? The ship sees me." It looked as if the ship were altering course and heading toward me. I ran back to the wheel, snatched up my pareu and put it on. I grabbed the container of flares and picked up the oar with the red T-shirt tied onto it, and started madly waving the oar as I did a jig. "I'll be in Hawaii tonight. A haole's delight. All bathed and bright. No more fright."

"HEY! WAIT A MINUTE!" I shouted.

I dropped the oar and shot off another flare. Then I shot off a parachute flare and a second parachute flare.

"YOU CAN'T LEAVE. WHY ARE YOU LEAVING?" I yelled at the distant sillouette of the ship. "What can I do? I've got to stop them."

I found the mirror stashed in the mizzen mast binnacle and with the help of the sun started flashing signals.

The ship never altered course; it must have been an optical illusion or just my deep, deep desire to be found.

All I could do was stomp around the deck screaming obscenities: "GODDAMN IT! THIS IS INSANE. HERE I AM IN BROAD DAYLIGHT AND YOU CAN'T EVEN SEE ME. YOU STUPID SHIP! COULDN'T YOU SEE THE STUPID FLARES?" With that, I grabbed a winch handle and started beating on the boom until I could pound no more. I dropped the winch handle and picked up my half-eaten can of sardines and threw them overboard. I collapsed in the cockpit, sobbing.

"This is crazy. I'm crazy."

"You're not crazy."

"I am too," I screamed to the sky.

"You just counted your chickens before they hatched."

"I thought they saw me."

"Yes, you're right, they should have. Hold on, love. You're almost there."

Even though I was thinking it, I could not say it out loud or The Voice would annihilate me. But I wished with all my heart that we had never left Tahiti. I knew there was no point in thinking it, but I couldn't stop myself. Back in Tahiti I had Richard, that's all I ever wanted . . .

"Richard, I smell the earth. Do you?"

Richard sniffed the air deeply and smiled. "Yes, the air's pungent. I didn't realize crushed coral had such a dry, crisp scent."

The anticipation of the hustle-bustle of Tahiti, after spending so much time in remote villages, was thrilling. The idea of reaching land and the little pleasures to come, like going to the bureau de poste for our mail and eating hamburgers and fries, tantalized us. Calling home would be a treat. I looked forward to hearing the latest gossip of who's doing what, with whom, and how much everybody misses us. But our first order of business would be to check into customs. It didn't matter that we had originally checked into Hiva Oa three months ago: Tahiti is not part of the Marquesan Islands group or the Tuamotu Archipelago, but rather it is one of the Windward Islands of the Society Islands group. French Polynesia is comprised of the three island groups.

As we came into Papeete's harbor, our whole world changed in a matter of moments. Gas and diesel fumes tinged the air. Activity surrounded us—everything from the goings-on at the naval headquarters to a cruise ship full of people on an adventure, to yachts—some of which we recognized from the Marquesas and Tuamotus were secured to the quay. We motored around to get our bearings and put the dinghy in the water. Then, selecting a spot on the quay, we backed in, lining *Mayaluga* up with the rest of the boats.

"Ahoy, *Mayaluga*," came an enthusiastic shout from the quay. "How was your trip?"

"Fantastic," Richard yelled to Jean Pierre, the owner of *Rashaba*, a steel sloop that housed a family of four we had met in the Marquesas.

With the electronics shut down and our sailing gear stowed, we collected our passports and the boat's papers, pulled the stern in and jumped on shore.

The paved road, Boulevard Pomme, ran parallel with the quay. The noise of speeding cars, mopeds, bikes and people intimidated us somewhat, yet excited us too.

"My God," Richard said, "this place is a zoo."

The customs office was close by. We walked right in and handed over our passports to the stern-faced official. All of our personal papers and *Mayaluga*'s papers were in order, showing our bond had been posted in Hiva Oa. Checking in was once again a breeze. Now we were anxious to eat.

The boulevard was lined with les roulettes, small trucks, like catering trucks, that specialize in certain foods. Crossing the street we were torn by which roulette to eat at first. There were crepes, stir-fry over noodles, chicken and rice, ice cream, hamburgers, as well as steaks and fries, shish kebab—you name it.

"Man, it smells good," I said. "The first thing I'm going to get is a brochette."

"What's a brochette?"

Red sky in mourning

"A shish kebab."

"That sounds great. But I'm dying for a steak." Richard smiled and licked his lips.

I ate one shish kebab, a crepe and a double-decker chocolate chip–mint ice cream cone. Richard ate twice as much as I did. We felt like slugs when we finished. We knew walking to le bureau de poste would help work off a couple of calories.

At the post office we mailed the letters we had written on our way to Papeete from Makemo and collected eight letters from our general delivery address. Thrilled to have received so much mail, we decided not to call home until we had read the letters. We'd read them on Mayaluga, where we could relax, and then call home the next day.

At a supermarket we picked up some sesame crackers as well as a choice brie from the rows and rows of fresh cheese, and Richard spotted a merlot he swore I'd love. Walking back toward the boat, we stopped in at the open-air market for some tomatoes, a red onion and apples—a little snack for later!

Kicked back in the cockpit sipping the smooth, fruity merlot, I opened the earlier of two letters from my mom. Ah ha, she had met a man named Brian through some friends, and they had a lot in common because he also worked on boats. Only he did mechanical and electrical repair. She added that the brightwork business she had taken over from me was doing great.

My mom's second letter was posted two weeks after the first. She and Brian were planning a trip on his boat to Catalina. She wrote, "He could be the one." Good for Mom, I thought.

Richard opened a letter from his sister, Susie, and then one from his dad. His sister hoped we were well and not so distracted by our love that we'd make navigational mistakes! His father's letter was very positive. He said he checked the Atlas daily to imagine Mayaluga's progress. He hoped we hit fair winds and didn't get stuck too long in the doldrums. He wanted Richard to be sure to call as soon as we arrived in Tahiti. Richard smiled as he folded up the letter and put it away.

The letter from my dad said my little brother was growing like a weed. Carolyn, my stepmother, was busy trying to keep up with the little rascal. He went on to say the waves had been great and he had been getting some surfing in on his days off of work as a fireman.

My father, stepmother and brother

I could tell my grandparents' letter from my grandmother's perfect handwriting. A lot of company from the midwest had been visiting, she wrote—everybody loved California because of its good weather. They hoped the cruise was easy and told me to be sure and call collect when I got to a phone. P.S., she added, say hello to Richard.

Dan, who had crewed with me delivering the racing yacht to San Francisco, had also written a letter with Sandra, his wife. Richard opened their letter next. They were envious, wishing they were in French Polynesia instead of San Diego. They had decided to move to the desert.

My grandparents and I

"The desert?" I questioned Richard as he read.

"That's what the old sod wrote. He says they are going to open a store and sell sunglasses."

We burst out laughing. Guess it makes sense to sell sunglasses in the desert.

The next day we called home. Everyone was as glad to hear our voices as we were to hear theirs. There's nothing like touching home-base to warm the heart. My grandma said she was baking chocolate bread pudding for Grandpa, and I swear I could smell it over the phone.

We spent several days at the quay, beam to beam with the other yachts. Everyday we went to the post office to check for and to send mail. We spent hours in the open air market buying fresh fruit and vegetables, wanting one of everything and knowing there would be no way to eat it all. We even bought flowers for *Mayaluga*'s table.

And what a thrill to get blocks of ice and have cold milk on corn flakes in the morning with lots of sugar. I loved the smell of ice in the ice box as I lifted the lid, the chill of the air stinging my nostrils. What a relief to know the milk wouldn't go bad, or the fresh meat and chicken. I would not miss finding a sprouted mossy green mold smiling at me from a warm icebox every time I opened it. Ice was a luxury and, as every sailor without refrigeration knows, nothing to be taken for granted.

A couple of boats Richard and I had met in the Marquesas were lined up along the quay: *Fleur d' Ecosse* owned by Anne and Ronald Falconer; and *Skylark*, owned by Phil & Betty Perish. Whenever a captain and mate felt in the mood, they would invite the other sailors over for a potluck. A mélange of unusual bonnes bouches (treats) appeared; sea stories grew like fish stories.

Every evening the big canoes were launched at the waterfront to practice for the big race on Bastille Day. There were men's and women's teams, plus a relay team. The canoes sat twelve paddlers each. Richard and I would sit in the cockpit watching them practice around the harbor, and one evening Richard asked if he could go on a short jaunt if they had room for an extra man. They did, and when they dropped him off he was beat. "They're animals love. Endurance like I've never seen."

A few days before Bastille Day the energy in the town cracked like lightning. Competitors from all over French Polynesia arrived, as did vendors who set up booths for selling their local cuisine.

Music accompanied the sunrise on Bastille Day. All the artist and merchants were set up in the square raring to sell their hand-made quilts, paintings, carvings, baskets, jewelry and food.

At the track, gunnysack races and horse races were taking place. Traditional Polynesian dance competitions went on throughout the day. Richard and I bought tickets to sit in the stands and watch the competition between the dancers, who performed all over the world. All their costumes were different, from palm-frond skirts, pom-poms and pom-pom headgear, to bikini tops and waist-bands intricately adorned with shells and beads. Other dancers wore shell crowns and pareus with leis over their bikini tops and flowers in their hair. All the dancers were sexy yet elegant, their hands signing a message that tantalized the mind. The Tamure, a Tahitian dance, was especially sensual, with the men wildly flap-ping their knees as the women shook their hips to and fro as they danced closer and closer.

Eventually Richard and I went down to the waterfront to watch the canoe races. Thousands of people had lined up to scream for their favorite teams, and we joined them cheering for the team

Canoe racers at Papeete, Tahiti

Richard had accompanied on his rowing jaunt.

Throughout the day on the waterfront we met up with our yachting buddies. We sat drinking beer and watching the vast variety of people walk by. We partied till the wee hours of the morning. And even when Bastille Day was over it took another couple of days for the partying to subside. Ah, the Tahitians really know how to celebrate.

As I came out of my Tahitian daydream and watched the ship drop off the horizon, I decided I didn't care what The Voice said. I stood up and shouted like a mad woman: "WE SHOULD HAVE NEVER LEFT TAHITI. DO YOU HEAR ME RICHARD? WE—SHOULD—HAVE—NEVER—LEFT—TAHITI!"

"*I—HOPE—YOU—FEEL—BETTER—NOW,*" came the know-it-all Voice.

Chapter Sixteen

Hazana and Maeva Beach

I was restless. Thinking back to Bastille Day and all its excite-ment had left me feeling like a caged animal. I had nowhere to go but round and round the deck. I tried to take deep breaths to calm down and relax. My mood definitely did not fit the slow pace of traveling a mere knot across the sea.

"Tami, if you'll be honest with yourself, you'll remember you were ready for the festival to be over."

"You know Voice, you really can be a pain in the you-know-what . . ."

After all the festivities of Bastille Day, Richard and I finally found the never-ending noise and traffic at the quay to be too overwhelming. We were partied-out and decided we missed our private time together: Too often it seemed someone was yelling down from the quay, "Ahoy, *Mayaluga*," or rowing up and knock-ing on the hull, asking for "permission to come aboard."

We decided to go around to the quiet anchorage at Maeva Beach. Even though a huge hotel was located there, we knew it would still be more private than the quay.

Ten boats were moored at Maeva Beach when we pulled in. We dropped anchor, and both of us sighed deeply as the tran-quillity embraced us.

Open-air trucks painted in an array of colors or in a collage of bright flowers, passed through the hotel parking lot to pick up passengers for the ten minute ride to town. With Tahitian music blasting, we piled onto le truck and boogied on down the road. It was always a fun ride, as we never knew who or what we might be crammed up against.

We took many day trips on les trucks, going as far as they would take us to explore the island. There was no problem jumping off at any point to hike down to a deserted white sand beach to swim and snorkel.

I looked up my old friends Antoinette and Haipade Topa, whom I had met years ago when I was sailing on *Sofia*. They still worked in the local chandlery in town during the week. Richard and I would go out to their house in Mataiea on many weekends, often bringing something to share for lunch. A few times we spent the night. The family house which belonged to Antoinette's parents, was a modest place. When Antoinette married Haipade, they had built an addition onto her parents' house, separated from the house by a corridor. Most homes had add-ons like this to accommodate growing families.

Antoinette and Haipade's home was not far from the Musee Gauguin, and Richard and I took the opportunity to visit the museum. Paul Gauguin, an ex–Paris stockbroker, left France to sail to Papeete in 1891, at age forty-three. It took him sixty-three days to get to Tahiti, where he thought Papeete to be too much like Europe. In disgust, he moved from Papeete, which is on the northwest side of Tahiti, to Mataiea, which is on the south coast of Tahiti. There he rented a bamboo hut. For a year and a half he painted and carved while living with his fourteen-year-old Tahitian mistress. Two years later, he packed up his sixty-six paintings and a dozen carvings and went back to France to show his work. Even though the exhibition was a flop, it established his reputation as an artist.

Gauguin returned to Tahiti, broke and riddled with venereal disease, and settled in Punaauia along the west coast. While there, he failed at an attempt to commit suicide. In 1901, a Paris art dealer contracted with Gauguin to provide artwork. This contract gave him the funds to move to Hiva Oa in the Marquesas, where his eccentricities drove the clergymen and officials of Hiva Oa crazy. Gauguin died, practically an outcast from the islanders, at age fifty-three.

The museum had many of Gauguin's prints and carvings, yet not many were of the Polynesians for which he is so famous. Richard and I reflected on Gauguin's sad life as we strolled across the manicured museum grounds: Huge trees shaded the emerald lawns and the pumpkin-colored bird of paradise flowers provided a brilliant contrast.

Not long after we arrived at Maeva Beach, Richard was asked to repair a boat built with a ferro-cement hull like *Mayaluga*'s. Because he liked to keep busy and make money, he readily agreed. While Richard was at work, I painted *Mayaluga*'s interior and varnished her brightwork.

One day when Richard was rowing into work, he noticed a new boat in the bay flying a British flag. Her name was *Hazana*. Richard rowed closer and yelled a "tally-ho" to her owners. He told them he was the owner of *Mayaluga*, the other Brit boat in the bay. *Hazana*'s owners, Peter and Christine Crompton, were from Southampton, England, it turned out, which basically made them neighbors to Richard's family in Cornwall.

The Cromptons invited us for a drink late one afternoon. As we rowed up to *Hazana* , I was awed by her lines and size. She was a beautiful forty-four-foot Trintella, a yawl of van de Stadt's design, built by Anne Wever in Holland. Richard introduced me to Peter and Christine, and they gave us a tour of *Hazana*'s interior which was adorned like a five star hotel compared to *Mayaluga*'s interior. The Cromptons were an attractive couple, mid-fifties, and very friendly, not pretentious at all. Peter made us a round of drinks, and we sat in the spacious cockpit enjoying the hors d'oeuvres Christine had made. Richard and the Cromptons learned they had a couple of common acquaintances. We enjoyed the visit.

A few days later the Cromptons asked us over for dinner. Much to Richard's delight, Christine added an English flare to the Polynesian meal with a homemade mango chutney. After dinner Christine mentioned her father was ill and that they were thinking of returning to England. Peter wondered what the possibilities might be of finding a delivery crew to sail *Hazana* to California, as it would be more convenient for them to come and go from the United States when they wanted to visit Christine's father. We could tell they were quizzing us out about the job. They asked what sailing experience we had, and we told them what we had done separately and together. They were amazed to learn that between us, Richard and I had sailed over fifty thousand miles.

Back on *Mayaluga* Richard asked me how I'd feel about delivering *Hazana*. At first I wasn't interested—I wasn't ready to go back to the States. I wanted to keep traveling and make it to New Zealand before going home for a visit.

But Richard went ahead and told Peter we might be interested in delivering *Hazana* to San Diego—depending on the fee.

Richard and Peter met again and discussed the terms of *Hazana*'s delivery to San Diego, California. When Richard came home and told me we'd be paid ten thousand dollars and airline tickets—from San Diego to Europe, back to San Diego, and then back here to Tahiti—I perked up and got interested in the job. It really did seem to be too good to pass up. We could sail a long time on ten thousand dollars. Since I had never been to Europe the idea of spending Christmas in England sounded exciting. The Cromptons liked the idea of being back on *Hazana* for Christmas, which meant *Hazana* would not be left unattended once she reached the States. After England, Richard and I could fly to San Diego and then back to *Mayaluga* in Tahiti and continue on to New Zealand. What would four months be out of our lives? We agreed to deliver *Hazana*.

Peter and Christine made reservations to fly home. A couple of days before they left, we went through *Hazana* with them. Christine took me through the galley operations, showing me where cooking utensils were kept and food goods stored. Peter took Richard through the engine room, explaining *Hazana*'s little quirks and his personal preferences for treatment of the engine and electronic gear.

The next day we went back to *Hazana* and went through the topside gear, the sails and rigging. *Hazana* was a sophisticated boat with roller-furling headsails, self-tailing winches, electric winches for the sheets, the lines, in the cockpit and a hydraulic boom vang. She was easily worth $200,000 and I actually started getting excited about our journey north aboard her.

Peter shook Richard's hand heartily when he handed over *Hazana*'s keys and said: "Have a good crossing, and be safe."

"Not to worry, we'll treat her like our own," Richard assured him, smiling.

The Cromptons were all packed, their bags lined up on a seat locker; Richard helped Peter load the bags in their dinghy, which they motored to shore; we rowed behind them in our dinghy. Once on shore there were hugs good-bye and a promise, "We'll see you in San Diego." The Cromptons left for the airport.

Richard and I ran back down the beach where the dinghies were tied. I grabbed the painter to the Cromptons' dinghy first, noticing the disappointment on Richard's face. "Just kidding," I teased, and traded lines with him. I knew he was eager to try out the inflatable with its fifteen horsepower outboard.

Antoinette and Haipade agreed to watch *Mayaluga* for us while we were delivering *Hazana* to San Diego. They suggested we leave her moored in the small bay in front of their house in Mataiea. The bay could only hold a couple of boats and would be a safe anchorage for *Mayaluga* while we were gone.

Richard plotted the course from Maeva Beach to the private bay, timing our entry for a high slack tide. As we rounded the point, we zigzagged our way into the narrow sliver of a channel.

Richard took special care to set the anchor. We stripped off all the sails and stowed them below. He drained the fresh water pump and the head and shut off all the thru-hull valves.

From the dinghy I watched Richard slide *Mayaluga*'s hatch shut. He patted the top of the hatch a couple of times and said, "We'll be back soon, love." Then he climbed down into the dinghy, untied the painter and rowed us to shore.

When we left *Mayaluga* my back was turned to her as Richard rowed us to shore. I could not see his eyes through his sunglasses, but I knew they were misty.

Moving aboard *Hazana* was like moving into the honeymoon suite at a Hilton hotel. She had pressurized hot running water for showers and two heads on board, not to speak of the latest in electronics. The galley was a gourmet cook's delight with plenty of room below to move around. She also had miles of foredeck space, and a giant cockpit.

We provisioned in Tahiti, planning for a thirty-day crossing to San Diego. There were many leftovers from the Cromptons' provisioning, as well as the goods we had brought from *Mayaluga*. But now that we had refrigeration, we bought extra treats.

Richard returned to *Hazana* that afternoon carrying a large rectangular box, ornately wrapped. "What's that?" I asked curiously.

Handing the box to me and smiling broadly, he said, "Open it and see."

"Do you think it's my birthday?" I questioned.

"No."

"An anniversary?" I cringed, scanning my minds personal calendar.

"No."

I pulled on the scarlet ribbon, and the box yawned partially open. Lifting the lid, a mossy green hue glowed under thin ivory paper. Unfolding the tissue, I lifted out a slinky spaghetti-strapped dress. "For me?"

"Do you like it?"

"It's gorgeous," I purred as I stood and held the dress against me. It was a seafoam green silk that tapered at the waist and hit just above my knees. "But why?"

"For being you," he simply stated.

When I looked puzzled, he continued. "I saw it on a mannequin in a shop window. She looked just like you, waist-length blond hair, green eyes the color of glass and a perfect body. I knew it was meant for you."

Blushing, I said, "You're something else," and threw my arms around him, smothering him with kisses.

"Come on, let's get cleaned up. I've made dinner reservations at Le Belvedere. Should we walk or take a cab?" he questioned.

"Le Belvedere—wow. Let's walk. I want to show off my new dress."

The late afternoon heat spiraled up from the roadway. We walked as much in the shade as we could, enjoying the breeze that gently blew against our skin. We trekked into a valley and along a lush canyon that must have contained every shade of green ever created.

The restaurant's covered patio overlooked a spectacular canyon populated with exotic trees, shrubs and flowers. In the distance spread the frothy rolling sea.

Dinner was scrumptious. Very rich with coconut cream and butter. When the table was cleared Richard reached across and took my hand. I watched him fondle my fingers and then I looked into his eyes, seeing that candid blue gaze.

"I love you with all my heart, Tami. And I want to be with you forever."

"I hope so," I answered smiling, feeling a bit self-conscience as I wondered the purpose of his confession.

"Will you marry me?" he suddenly blurted out, slipping an intricately knotted white twine ring on my finger.

"It's lovely. Did you make it?"

"Yes. Later I'll get you the real thing. Whatever you'd like."

I shook my head no. "Nothing can ever be as precious as this." My eyes brimmed.

"What's wrong? Don't you want to marry me?"

"Yes—yes, I want to marry you. I'd marry you this second."

"Gees, Tami, for a minute I thought you were going to say no."

"No? Are you crazy? I'd be crazy to say no."

We dreamily walked back to the boat. I wondered out loud how my new name, Mrs. Richard Sharp, would sound. Or Tami Sharp. Or Richard and Tami Sharp. Richard said, "It sounds just right."

Back on *Hazana* we turned on slow music and danced for a spell in each other's arms. I suddenly felt like a woman, not a girl. A woman soon to be a "wife." Romance rocked *Hazana* that night.

The next day I woke up a new woman—an engaged woman. With everything in order we took off for Moorea on a shakedown cruise. We dropped anchor and stayed on board *Hazana* that night, enjoying her luxury and watching the beautiful sunset from her spacious cockpit.

The next day we went ashore to find Heftsy, a woman I had heard of who made beautiful batiks. Taking the Cromptons' folding bikes and a packed lunch to shore, we biked up the Opunohu Valley and discovered a wonderful spot where we could see both the ocean and the valley. We sat eating lunch in the serene beauty. Once finished, we biked on to Heftsy's. She was home and happy to show us her unique batiks of local people. Most were of women with bright flowers in their hair. The batiks were brilliantly colored and often worn as pareus by locals. They would make great wall hangings too, so we purchased six to take home for gifts.

On our peddle back to *Hazana*, the wind started to pick up and soon became a steady blow. By the time we reached the bay *Hazana* was anchored in, she had drug anchor and was almost aground on a small motu. We dropped the bikes, dragged the dinghy into the water and raced out to her. Scrambling topside I ran to the bow, wrapped the anchor line around the drum on the windlass and started to pull as Richard got the engine started. We changed positions, and Richard raised the anchor as I steered us away from land. We motored out of the wind, but stayed in the same bay and reanchored. Richard went ashore to retrieve the bikes and batiks, and I stayed on *Hazana* to make sure she didn't drag again.

With *Hazana* ready to go, we were too. There was nothing left to do, we contemplated leaving Tahiti early for the crossing to California. We had studied the weather forecasts carefully: No storms were forecast, so we felt pretty confident we would be safe as far as the weather was concerned. We estimated we could make good time sailing from the southern hemisphere into the northern hemisphere, and as it was well past the middle of hurricane season and the occurrence of storms at this time of the year was statistically low, we decided to go for it. We felt indestructible—we knew our love would conquer all.

We left Moorea and went back to Papeete to top off the fuel, water and propane tanks. We checked out of Papeete at 1330 hours, September 22. As *Mayaluga* was remaining in Tahiti, and we were returning within four months, our bonds remained posted. We took off for America.

Chapter Seventeen

Glow Sticks and Milkshakes

If only this were a shakedown cruise and I could turn around and start over.

"Don't go there," The Voice cut in.

One of *Hazana*'s two batteries had been thrown out of its Plexiglas casing during the capsize, but by a miracle it had landed right side up, undamaged. If it had landed any other way, I probably would have been painfully, perhaps fatally burned by acid-contaminated water before I came to. The other battery, still in its casing, was also undamaged.

I used battery power only at night, to light up the two cockpit compasses—one in the binnacle, the other on the cockpit bulkhead. When the first battery finally ran out of juice, I switched to the second one, realizing it might also give out before I reached safety.

It was Day Thirty-Five. I estimated I was still one hundred forty-five miles from Hawaii. To conserve even more battery power I started using glow sticks that I had found while cleaning below.

That night I cracked my first one. The lime green light sparkled like magic in my hand. It reminded me of when I was a kid and we'd go to the beach at night to see the slender, silvery grunion run. Waves would cast the grunion on shore and we'd run up and down the soft wet sand waving our glow sticks like pirates wave their swords.

Sometimes I would sneak away from the other kids and hide near the pier at the water's edge. I'd let my feet sink in the quicksand until I felt that first crusty edge of a sand crab's claw. Then I'd leap back and run for my life, screaming at the top of my lungs, "The crabs are coming. The crabs are coming." I'd run as fast as I could past the other children, and sure enough they'd start screaming and running too.

Holding the glow stick up to the starless night, I started writing in the sky. I wrote Richard's name, over and over and over. I scribbled a rolling "R," with a flourish at the end of the "D."

Facing the bow and pointing the wand straight ahead, I commanded: "Love—come to me," and slowly brought the wand to my heart. Turning starboard I grasped the wand to my heart and repeated my order, "Come to me." Feeling the wind freshen on my left cheek, I checked the compass and altered course a degree. I did an about-face to the stern and the path I had just traveled, and said in a deep voice, "Richard, let your spirit come to me." Gracefully turning portside, I stretched my right arm out as far as I could, and then gradually brought the wand to my breast, repeating the mantra: "Come to me."

Dazzled by the feeling of power, even though Richard's spirit didn't come to me, I set the glow stick on top of the binnacle. I glanced at my heading and shifted the wheel a couple of degrees. Feeling omnipotent, I expanded my commands: "Bring me a milkshake. It has to be from Baskin-Robbins, you know, 31 Flavors, and it must be mint-chocolate-chip." The craving became too much, and the spell broke. "Oh man, what I wouldn't do for a milkshake right now."

"Stop it. Don't be ridiculous. You know you can't have a milkshake."

"Haven't you ever wanted a milkshake?"

"Of course I have. But this fantasy is pointless."

"Maybe you have no imagination."

"Maybe I don't like to put myself through unnecessary pain."

The Voice had no sense of humor, I discovered. I pretended to drink my mint-chocolate-chip milkshake. "Ummm. Oh man, this is good. Ummm. I can hardly stand how refreshed the mint makes my mouth feel."

"Cool?"

"Very cool"

176

The Voice hesitated, *"May I have some?"*
"Sorry, it's all gone," I said, tossing the invisible cup overboard.
"Oh man . . ."
"Next time you should grasp the joy of fantasy."

For the next few days the wind was fluky. I cursed the devil for this.

The sun woke me on Day Thirty-Eight. I couldn't stay under the blanket any longer. I had been awake most of the night, steering. If only I could sleep in, have breakfast in bed.

I sat up and stretched. As I headed for the bow to check the rig, I looked around and stopped short. "It can't be—can it?" I squinted my eyes, trying to focus. It's got to be."

On the horizon I saw an isolated cloudlike shape. Could it be Hawaii? I went back to the wheel, and for an hour I steered toward the granite-colored smudge in front of me. Finally I couldn't deny it. I was seeing land. It had to be the island. Hawaii was right where I thought it should be. A great relief flooded over me. My spine seemed to melt as I laid my head in my lap and cried.

After a short while I calmed down and was overcome by a feeling of awe. But what exactly am I in awe of, I wondered. Land? People? Home? Could it just be the reality that lay in front of me? Yes, everything I had been wanting was here. Well, almost everything. . . Suddenly excitement surged through me, and I stood up and shouted: "LAND—LAND HO!" Then I danced about like a warrior, quickly wearing myself out. "This calls for a celebration. Beer! My last beer, the one I've been saving for this moment. And a cigar. "YAHOO!"

Scrambling below I sought out a beer and a cigar. Topside, I climbed on the boom, lit the cigar and popped open the bottle. "Oh God, I'm so excited. And grateful. I'm so very, very grateful. Thank you. Thank you. Amen." I hadn't felt grateful for anything in over a month, well, except for the fresh water, cigars, beer and moisturizer. It felt good to feel so positive, so alive.

"I know my mom will come and get me. They'll help me with all this." But what can they really do, I thought? Hold my hand? It will be up to me to get organized, to notify everyone, to try to explain how it happened—why it happened. My positive feeling waned.

"What will I tell Richard's family?" Fear gripped me. "How will I tell them?" I involuntarily shook my head. "How will I be able to tell anyone about Richard?" Emotion choked me.

"And the Cromptons, this beautiful boat of theirs." *Hazana*, poor *Hazana*. *Hazana* who saved my life. The Cromptons will be devastated too. "I'm sorry," I rehearsed, growing sadder. "We did our best. We did." They'll just have to believe me. Tears streamed down my face. "I've done my best too." The last drop of the hot beer muffled another sob.

"Oh God, what are people going to think of me? Look at me—I'm a wreck. I've lost so much weight, and my hair—my hair used to be so pretty. If one person looks at me funny, I'm gonna crack. I'm on a thin keel as it is. Oh God, I'm so scared."

I could feel adrenaline surging through my body. I was afraid to see people again, to get back into society. What was going on? Did I want to stay out here forever, drifting into oblivion? Maybe it would be easier than explaining how it was that I lived and Richard got sucked into the bowels of the sea. His parents will wish I had been the one at the wheel. My parents, though sad, will be glad I wasn't. Will anyone realize it would have been better if both of us had died?

"You're regressing. You were not meant to die. How many times do I have to tell you, Richard's time was up and yours is not. Just know everyone will be glad you are home and safe."

The Voice was like a warm blanket thrown over my shoulders. I wanted to believe The Voice; I needed to believe The Voice. "I'm so scared."

"I know you are. And you have every right to be."

"You wouldn't be scared."

"I might be. But one thing I know for sure, is that I'd be happy I was not going to be alone anymore."

"I'm happy for that. Really, I am."

"You're not acting happy, dry those eyes. That's a girl."

"I suppose you'll leave me now too."

"No, I will never leave you. I will always be here when you really need me."

"Where do you live?"

"I live in your soul."

"Like a soul-mate? Or guardian angel?"

"Yes, something like that."

The Voice and I sat quietly for a while. I felt totally at peace. Finally I sighed and announced: "Well, there's not a breath of wind up here; guess I better get her shipshape." And with that I crawled down off my perch and went below.

Chapter Eighteen

De Plane—Insane

Down below, *Hazana* didn't look shipshape by any means, but it was the best I could do. I was sitting at the chart table cleaning the connectors on the VHF radio when I heard an engine. "What the..." I clambered topside.

Shading my eyes I looked around. The sound was coming from the sky; a plane. A military plane. A low-flying military plane! As quickly as I could, I shot off four flares. I grabbed the oar with the red T-shirt on it and waved and waved. The plane never even dipped its wing. I felt stunned. How in the hell could it not see me? Where's the island? All of a sudden the island was gone. "Where's the damn island?"

I looked at the palms of my hands and turned them over. They looked like hands. I put my palms up to my cheeks and felt my face. It felt like a face. I licked the fingers of my right hand and rubbed my thumb over them. It was wet, sort of sticky. All of a sudden I slapped myself in the face. First with my right hand and then with my left. I kept slapping myself, until finally I screamed at the top of my lungs: "AHHHHHHHHHHHHHH. I'M DEAD. I'M DEAD. IT'S ALL A TRICK. I'VE BEEN DEAD ALL ALONG." My knees gave way, and I collapsed onto the seat. "This is hell. I'm in hell. Hell, is this limbo? Is this the devil's trick? Not knowing what's real? I'm not real. No one sees me. No one saves me. It's going to be like this forever. What did I do that was so bad? All I did was go below like Richard told me. It's not my fault."

Standing up, I waved my fist to the heavens. "DO YOU HEAR ME, GOD? IT'S NOT MY FAULT. I'M SICK OF ALL THE GUILT. I'M SICK OF THE NIGHTMARES. YOU MADE THE HURRICANE. YOU KILLED RICHARD. AND YOU MADE ME SURVIVE. HOW COULD

YOU? WHAT IS SO MERCIFUL ABOUT YOU, GOD, THAT YOU KILLED RICHARD AND PUT ME IN THIS HELL-HOLE? WELL, I'LL TELL YOU SOMETHING, I'M NOT STAYING HERE. I'M GOING TO SHOOT MY BRAINS OUT. THEN I WON'T BE ABLE TO WORRY ABOUT A GODDAMNED THING. TO HELL WITH THE ISLAND AND TO HELL WITH YOU!"

Hysterically, I dashed below and rummaged through a locker until I found the rifle and shells. I loaded the rifle and, leaning against the nav station, tried to cram the barrel into my mouth. The cold metal cracked against my teeth. "Ouch. Come on damn it."

I moved toward the settee, thinking that maybe if I sat down I wouldn't shake so much and the metal wouldn't rattle so violently against my teeth.

"Tami, you know you can't take your own life now."

"WHAT ARE YOU TALKING ABOUT?" I slammed down the butt of the rifle on the cabin sole. "I'M DEAD. I'M ALREADY DEAD! IT'S JUST MY BRAIN THAT ISN'T DEAD. MY IMAGINATION IS GOING ON AND ON AND ON. THERE IS NO RELIEF! I CAN'T STAND IT ANYMORE."

"Tami, you're close. You're so close. Believe in yourself. Remember the prayer you love about God's big sea and your small boat. Tami, your boat is small, it is hard to see. You know that. Put the rifle down. Believe in yourself. Don't give up the ship, girl. Go look. I dare you. Come on, I double dare you. The island is real, it's not an illusion. It is Hawaii. You're almost there. I promise—I promise. Go look—please, go look."

Chagrined, I let the rifle drop and leaped topside. The island was there, bright and clear.

"Ohmigod, what did I almost do?" I clung to the boom to stop myself from shaking.

I almost gave up. I almost killed myself. I'm just so tired and lonely, I'm going crazy.

Letting go of the boom, I jumped down into the cockpit. I plunged my hands into the five-gallon bucket of saltwater and splashed big scoops of the cool water over my face.

"Oooh." It felt good. Not cold, but wet and real. I did it again. Then I stretched my arms high, and as I lowered them I roared like a lioness: "AAAAAAAAAAAAAAAAHHHHH!

Staring at the island my mind worked overtime: Believe in yourself, Tami. You heard The Voice. You made it this far. You don't need anyone or anything to save you. You must keep the faith, trust The Voice and know there's a reason you lived.

I sat there a moment feeling my nerves unfray before I had to finally admit, "I was meant to save myself."

Chapter Nineteen
Hold On, Hold On

That night I woke up to a heavy rain and building wind. The compass needle was all over the place. All I could do was keep the wheel lashed and pull a waterproof cover over me and my cockpit bed, and go back to sleep. I was exhausted.

When I was able to take my first sight the next day, my plotting showed I had been set north, pushed off my course by twenty-five miles. I could no longer see the island. I made a conscious decision to stay awake and tend the wheel constantly. That night I went into the galley in search of a stimulant. The best I could come up with was a cold cocoa-coffee drink. I filled a thermos with the mixture and took it to the cockpit.

And so, on my Forty-First day alone at sea I sailed to within a few miles of Hilo Harbor. At 0130 in the morning the lights in the bay beckoned me, but I dared not go closer because of the huge reef that stretched far off shore. With a glow stick I studied the illustrated chart of Hilo Harbor I had found in an old book. The words, "Not for navigational purposes," stood out. Oh, how I wanted to ignore them and get to those lights, some real food, real people, a shower and some decent sleep. But only a fool or a sailor with local knowledge would attempt the entrance at night. It was just too tenuous. I had to keep reminding myself that I hadn't gone through all this to end up on a reef now.

So, in the early morning I tacked back and forth just off the entrance to Hilo Harbor. I was so near and yet still so far. Couldn't I just be there? No, I couldn't. I felt so confused. I knew I was a changed woman, never to be that innocent carefree girl again. I was scared of the humanity only a couple of miles away. Yet, I was excited too. Tears poured down my face.

"These tears—where are they coming from?" I asked The Voice.

"These are different tears, Tami. These tears are tears of joy."

"But it's wrong to feel joy. I should be sad. I am still sad. I miss Richard so much."

"You will always miss Richard, and you will always love Richard. But life goes on, Tami. You have to believe in yourself. Richard's time was up, and yours wasn't. You survived because you are you. Not everyone would have made it. Be proud, woman. You've mourned what would easily be equivalent to a year's worth, in all these days you've been alone. Feel joy, you deserve it. Soon you'll be with people who love you and you'll be smothered by all the love you've been missing."

"But it won't be the same."

"It will be what you make of it. Another man will come when you are ready, and he will love you as deeply as Richard did."

"But will I be able to love him as much as I loved Richard?"

"Yes. In time your heart will open and be eager to love again. Believe in yourself, in what your heart tells you."

"I'm going to miss you."

"I'm always here."

"Are you God?"

The Voice never answered. Maybe there is no answer. But my heart told me that The Voice was some sort of higher power.

Early morning crept along extremely slow. I knew it would be my last few hours at sea, my last hours to be alone. I wondered who my first contact would be? A fishing boat? A private yacht?

Glancing to port, the pastel lights along the mountainside of Hilo, Hawaii, were beginning to go out one by one. Hold on Tami, hold on . . .

I couldn't help but ask myself again, as I had a million times already: Why? Why hadn't I realized we were vunerable? That one or both of us could die out here in the middle of the ocean?

But the core of my being shouted back in defense: Because you were fearless, Richard was fearless. It was true I had concentrated on tropical isles and white sandy beaches, warm water, perfect waves, exotic ports and love.

I finally had to admit that nothing could have kept me from the sea.

I looked at my star friends in the sky and said a farewell to each constellation that had so graciously entertained me and guided me on this long, slow voyage. The W in the sky was for water, but it still stood for wondrous to me. Wondrous and wonderful Richard. Wondrous and wonderful that I had made it. I knew the stars would never be as outstanding on land as they are out here at sea.

I grabbed Richard's flowered shirt to my heart and desperately confessed: "I love you. You know I love you. I love you with all my heart." It was all I could say. I could not look at the lapis lazuli sea without seeing his eyes. I could not say that final good-bye. I stuffed his shirt inside mine, next to my heart, and reached for the twine ring on my finger that Richard had given me.

As dawn strolled aimlessly across the sky, I took a deep breath and readied *Hazana* for the harbor entry.

At the bow I heaved the anchor out of its locker and then pulled all the chain and rode onto the deck. I wanted the anchor and chain ready in case *Hazana* ended up being blown toward the reef or shore.

I hoisted the American red, white and blue flag on the jury rigged portside shroud as a courtesy flag and then automatically hoisted the yellow quarantine flag under it as all sailors learn to do when crossing international waters and entering a new port. I

Research vessel, Hokusei Maru

dug out, from down below, *Hazana*'s English home-port flag. As I unfurled it, I tried to brush out the mildew and wrinkles. I stuck the flag in it's holder on the stern rail, remembering how proud Richard was of his citizenship.

I went back to the wheel and altered course for the harbor entrance. No sooner had I done this than I noticed a large ship also heading for the harbor entrance. I grabbed the flare gun and started shooting.

The ship seemed to pause.

I shot off a couple more flares and then grabbed the oar with the faded red T-shirt. At the bow, I waved it evenly back and forth, not frantically as I had all the unsuccessful times before.

Suddenly the vessel flashed its running lights and altered course.

My God, they see me. They actually see me. I didn't know what to do. I felt as if I should do something, but what? They were approaching fast. What will I say? "Hello, my name is Tami Oldham, and this is the sailing yacht *Hazana*. I've been like this for a long time . . ."

Hazana started to rock as the looming ship reversed its engines and slowed down, sending forward its bow wake. I was afraid it would ram me. It was huge, two hundred feet or so. It cast a dark shadow over *Hazana*. Faces, Asian and American, were peering over the rail intently staring down at me. I felt exposed and vulnerable. Suddenly, one of the seventy-five or so men on board shouted at me. I could barely hear him through the

rumble of the engines now grumbling in neutral gear. "ARE YOU ALL RIGHT?" He yelled.

I nodded yes and then burst out crying. Through my sobs I felt the pity in the eyes watching me. I heard some shouts and, looking up, saw nodding heads and smiles of encouragement. "IT'S OKAY. WE'LL HELP YOU. YOU'LL BE FINE," shouted the spokesperson.

As I gained control of myself, I heard him ask: "HAS SOME-ONE DIED?"

Again, I nodded yes.

"IS THAT THE BODY?" questioned the officer, pointing to the orange inflatable dinghy rolled up and lashed down on the port aft-quarter.

Baffled, I shook my head no.

"WE'VE NOTIFIED THE COAST GUARD. DO YOU NEED ANY-THING?"

Retrieving the tow line.

I needed everything, but I shook my head no and grasped the bow pulpit harder. *Hazana* was really rocking back and forth.

Soon someone swung a glass container, tied on a line, down to me from the deck of the vessel. I nodded my thank you. Untying it proved very difficult with my weak and nervous hands. I could smell the hot coffee before I tasted it. My taste buds had forgotten the satisfying coating the mouth gets from hot coffee's bitter bean. I set the coffee down and someone threw me an apple. It seemed like forever since I had tasted an apple. As I bit into it, the soft juice rolled down my chin. It tasted much sweeter than I remembered.

It was a great effort for the large vessel to stand off of tiny *Hazana*, and it had been standing by for what seemed like an hour waiting for the Coast Guard.

"WE'RE GOING TO PASS YOU A TOWLINE," came an announcement suddenly.

There was a shout from up above, and then a monkey's fist was thrown down to me. I caught it and pulled in all its excess line, finally getting to the hawser attached to it. The hawser was huge— two inches in diameter. I could barely get it on board; it weighed a ton, the type of rope you'd use to tow another

ship, not a sailboat. I couldn't decide where to tie the monstrosity. Finally, I decided to wrap it around the anchor windlass. Once it was secured, I yelled "GO SLOW—SLOW!" and waved my hands, palms down, in front of me.

As the ship's engines roared, I held on tight. The cover on the anchor windlass broke into pieces, but the windlass itself was held by two of its four bolts, as *Hazana* was jerked forward. Quickly we seemed to be galloping across the swells. The slowest the ship could go was probably the fastest *Hazana* had ever gone. We were moving at least ten knots in nothing flat. It took all my concentration steering *Hazana* behind the ship. I could feel all the faces still watching me. All I could think about was stay on track—stay on track.

The ship towed me inside the reef, where I stood off with help from the current. Soon the Coast Guard arrived in their twenty-six-foot auxiliary boat. I cast off the ship's hawser and secured the lines the Coast Guard passed to me, side-tying *Hazana* to the side rail of the Coast Guard runabout.

Inside Radio Bay was a concrete quay. The Coast Guard towed me to it, and I tied up to another Coast Guard boat moored there. Then two Coast Guard officials came on board. One was Petty Officer Rodenhurst, who was exceptionally kind to me. I kept crying and couldn't talk in complete sentences. I'm sure I was in shock.

Also moored in the quay was the blue hulled sloop *Tamarii*

Richard and I had seen in the Marquesas. As I glanced its way, I could see the owners watching the Coast Guard tow me in. The woman, Helga, yelled to me, "WHEN YOU ARE DONE, COME OVER TO THE BOAT."

Petty Officer Rodenhurst gently said to me a number of times that they had a shower I could use. I needed a shower, but I wasn't ready for the isolation. I needed human contact.

I was very anxious to go to the *Tamarii* and talk to fellow cruisers, or at least people I felt I could relate to and who could relate to me. I told the Coast Guard men a condensed version of what had happened, enough for them to get the picture and that there was no way I needed an ambulance or the hospital. They told me they would need to take a written statement in a while, but to go ahead and visit my friends.

When I got to *Tamarii*, a feast awaited me. Eggs, ham, roast beef, cheese, potato salad, sweet breads, milk, juice, coffee. I sat down and poured my heart out. I ate and cried, and cried and ate, and eventually laughed a time or two. The German couple were fascinated with my story and they asked me questions and I answered as we talked and talked. They offered me a cigarette, and gave me a snifter of brandy. All their nurturing helped to calm me, to feel at one with humanity again.

A couple hours had passed when Petty Officer Rodenhurst came knocking on the hull. "Tami, we need to take that statement now. Okay?"

I left *Tamarii* with more tears but with a newfound strength. "Would you like to get a change of clothes so you can shower?" Rodenhurst asked.

"Yes, yes . . . "

It wasn't until the hot water was streaming down my back that I realized why the petty officer had kept saying to me, that I might want to take a shower. I could feel each day I had spent at sea shedding off of my skin, layer by layer. My hair was completely dreadlocked, and there wasn't a thing I could do to untangle it. I still had a scab on my leg from the deep cut, but the wound on my head was almost healed. All the other wounds had healed. All but the wound to my heart. My body was lean, bony, skinny. Too skinny for me.

At the sink I brushed my teeth over and over; the cigars had stained them. I stared at the dark circles under my eyes and the angry-looking scar on my head as I brushed my teeth. Slowly even my teeth brightened to their natural white. If only I could brush my soul free of the pain that had so deeply stained it.

As I went back into the office I could see from the men's eyes that they were looking at a female—a female survivor, not a ravaged victim anymore.

After the written report was complete, Petty Officer Rodenhurst told me he was a newlywed and that he and his wife and daughter had an extra room in their house if I'd like to spend the night there, and to please call him Chris.

"Thank you, I'd—yes." I don't think I could have spent another night on *Hazana* now that I was clean and on land.

Chapter Twenty
On Solid Ground

Perry Rodenhurst, Chris's wife, came to the station with her six-year-old stepdaughter, Shannon, to pick me up. Perry was in her mid-twenties, attractive and lean, with blond shoulder-length hair. She was very gentle with me.

At their lovely home Perry showed me into the den, where she tugged at the seat in the couch, unfolding it into a bed. She told me to make myself at home and pointed out the telephone. As Perry closed the door, she said to take my time with my calls.

I sat down on the edge of the bed and looked around the cozy room—a desk, framed family photographs and books. How stable and normal it all seemed. Taking a deep breath I picked up the phone and dialed the operator to call my mother collect. Her number was busy. I tried my dad. No answer. I tried my mom again—still busy.

I was starting to lose it. Couldn't my mom feel my need to talk to her? It never dawned on me to ask the operator to make an emergency break through to my mother's number.

My grandparents had to be home, it was early evening, Pacific Standard Time. But what if they weren't? I wouldn't be able to stand it. I had to talk to someone—now.

My grandfather answered on the fourth ring. "Yellow."

"Grandpa, it's me. How are you?"

"How is *me*? How is *you*?"

"Oh, Grandpa, I'm not so good," I started sobbing. "Richard is—is dead . . ." Thus, my highly emotional phone call began. I started sobbing.

Eventually my grandmother got on the line. I had to keep repeating myself because grief muffled my words. My mind was tired, confused and still scared. *Now what? Now what?* pounded inside my brain. I'm sure I sounded crazy; I felt crazy.

After talking with my grandparents, I tried my mom again. Her number was still busy. I decided to call Richard's sister, Susie, in England. Jurrick, her husband, answered and told me she wasn't home. I sadly managed to give him the news in fairly accurate order. With both of us distraught and crying, Jurrick told me he had known Richard since he was a boy, that they were more than brothers-in-law. He was very upset, but volunteered to phone Richard's parents and let them know. I assured him I would call again, later.

I decided to call *Hazana*'s owners, the Cromptons, that instant and get it over with. My hand shook violently as I tried to dial the number. Peter answered the phone. "Peter? A terrible thing has happened," I babbled. "Oh, this is Tami. You know Tami . . . We got caught in the hurricane. Richard went overboard. He's gone." I barely took a breath between sentences. "*Hazana*'s masts are gone, she's a wreck. But she's floating."

"Oh dear, oh dear, oh no," Peter kept saying.

I had told the story so many times by now that my voice was almost flat, losing emotion, relying on logic. "*Hazana* will probably be considered totaled. You should contact your insurance company. Excuse me? Oh, I'm in Hilo. Hilo, Hawaii."

I could hear the devastation in Peter's voice as he told me how sorry he was to hear about Richard, that they had liked him so much. It was considerate of Peter not to question me about *Hazana*'s condition. All he said was that he and Christine would come immediately to Hawaii.

I finally got through to my mother. Her voice on the end of the line sent me into a tailspin. I could barely say "Mom . . ."

"Tami? My God, where have you been?" Her familiar chastise was a blessing. "I have been worried sick about you. I've gone to the Coast Guard station twice—where are you?"

"Oh Mom . . ."

"Honey? What is it? Are you okay?"

"Mom . . ." I must have sobbed for ten minutes before her

soothing, knowing voice could get me under control. We had a long, long discussion. She assured me over and over that Richard's death and the destruction of *Hazana* weren't my fault.

Finally, I was speechless. My mom insisted I give her the Rodenhursts' phone number. She was going to call the airport to book a flight immediately, and then she'd call me back. Her voice saying, "I love you, honey," echoed over and over as I lay down on the bed and waited for her to call back.

Shortly thereafter, she did; she'd be arriving in eleven hours. Would I be okay? Did I need anything? She wanted to talk to Perry. I said, "No. Just talk to me." So we talked on and on, until finally she said I should get some rest.

I laid down and stared at the white ceiling. Soon its flat surface became the sea rolling softly to the corners of the room, sailing down the decorated walls. My body, though stationary, rocked back and forth, back and forth. A light rapping on the door startled me. When I turned to look, Perry had opened it and peeked in. I hadn't slept. I wanted to, but my mind wouldn't relax. She invited me to join them for dinner.

At the table, Shannon had obviously been told not to ask me any questions, but I could tell she was full of them by the way she stared at me and stroked her hair.

After a light meal, we all gathered around the television to watch the movie *Airplane*. As I sat in a comfortable bean-bag chair, my mind kept wondering how one minute I could be stranded at sea and the next be in front of a television, watching a slapstick catastrophe movie. Somehow it all didn't make sense.

I couldn't make it through the movie, so I excused myself and went to bed, but I still couldn't sleep. I decided to try to reach my dad again. He answered.

"Dad?"

"Tami! Honey. Great timing we just got in."

"Dad . . ."

"Hun, what's wrong? Are you okay? Where are you? We've been waiting to hear from you? "

"Dad . . ." I burst out crying, "Richard's gone."

"What do you mean Richard's gone?"

"Gone! The boat's trashed, and Richard's tether broke and he's dead."

"Oh my God!"

"That's what Richard said, and then the boat capsized. When I came to, he was gone."

"Oh, honey, where are you?"

"Hilo, Hawaii. I just got here today."

"I'll come right over? I can get there . . ."

"No, it's okay, Mom's on her way." We talked for about an hour. Having to relive everything over and over was grueling, but healing too.

After we hung up, I was spent. I caught a glimpse of myself in the dresser mirror and tried to comb my fingers through my hair, but there was no way to put a dent in the tangles. I gave up. All night long I tossed and turned, falling in and out of sleep. I wanted Richard, and I wanted the sun to come up. I wanted my mom to get there and take me home, take me away from all this and all that would inevitably still come. I wanted to get on with my life and have all this behind me. Yet, I knew there were things I had to do first. I could not escape.

Most of the night I stared at the pearlized reflections of the moon sweeping the wall and ceiling of the bedroom. Somehow I felt more trapped being inside a house, than I had felt outside stranded on a boat.

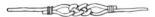

The next morning I felt eager to return to *Hazana*. I missed her. Chris had already left for work. Perry, trying to help me feel better about my appearance, gave me a dress to wear and helped me hide my hair under two stylishly tied bandannas. She told me I looked better in the dress than she did, and even though I knew

I looked odd being so thin and all, I appreciated the comment, the confidence she was trying to instill in me.

We dropped Shannon off at school, and then Perry drove me to the Coast Guard station. When I went inside, Chris asked me if I'd seen all the reporters outside. "No," I said, anxiously.

News channel, newspaper and magazine reporters had lined the quay, waiting for me to show up. Chris escorted me out and stood by as I was interviewed. The reporters asked me to move here and there for the benefit of the cameras and videos. I was totally blown away by all the attention and spent an hour and a half trying to accommodate the media: smiling, smiling, smiling as if everything were a-okay now. See how good I am, how cooperative. I had no idea my ordeal at sea would cause such a stir.

After the reporters left, I escaped inside *Hazana*. There I let myself go and cried from deep down in my soul as I sat alone, looking at the shambles anew. What should I do? I didn't know what to do or where to go from here, or where to start.

Finally the time came for me to take a cab to the airport and meet my mother. Standing at the gate I was not surprised to see that my mom was the first passenger to disembark. She came rushing out and scooped me up in her arms. Hugging me, squishing me, crying all over me. She rocked me back and forth for the longest time and let me cry, and cry, while she cried with me. Many heads turned. They had no idea what a miracle this reunion was.

Brian, my mom's boyfriend, guided us out of the mainstream of foot traffic, and finally as Mom and I calmed down, she introduced me to him. We hugged hello. There were tears of compassion in his blue eyes. Blue eyes—I had to look away.

We took a cab into town and checked into a nice hotel not too far from the quay. After lunch and a lot of talking and more crying, Mom decided we would deal with my dreadlocks first. The beauty salon at the hotel said they couldn't do anything about my matted tresses but cut them off. I burst into tears. We tried another beauty shop and they callously said they would have to shave my head. I was not going to let anyone cut off all my hair;

Three beauticians worked for two days de-tangling my hair

my identity was shattered as it was. I'd spend the rest of my life combing the snarls out if I had to.

Searching for another beauty salon we came across the House of Lantz. My mom firmly explained what had happened to me and how it could be to the salon's advantage to help us because of the interest the media had in my story. They agreed to try. As I was tilted back in the comfortable chair, my head was slathered with conditioner and detangler. I sat for four hours holding my scalp as three beauticians combed out the snarls as gently as they could. It hurt like hell. They stopped for the day when I could take no more. The next day I went back, and they worked on the opposite side. My scalp ached from all the tugging, but I wouldn't let them stop. After another four hours my hair hung long and straight. My mom held my cheeks, looked deeply into my eyes and said, "There's my beautiful baby girl." Finally, I started to feel like me. I couldn't thank House of Lantz enough.

The Cromptons arrived the next day. I nervously paced the airport's waiting area for their plane. Now, as they hugged me hello, I started weeping. We went directly to *Hazana*.

As we walked up to *Hazana*, all I could hear was Christine saying, "Oh no. Oh no." Peter was very quiet. Even with *Hazana* directly in front of their eyes, they still couldn't believe the damage.

"It's amazing she didn't sink," Peter said.

We sat in the cockpit, and I retold the whole story again. I tried to answer all their questions. Some explanations I could state clearly; others cracked the foundation, and a flood of tears escaped. Peter had his camera and took a lot of pictures. Christine appeared most overwrought. I had no control over my emotions and simply sat there, an endless stream of tears rolling down my face.

My mother came to *Hazana*, and I introduced her to the Cromptons. Seeing how upset I was and emotionally drained, she became the "Mama Bear," insisting I come back to the hotel and rest. I went back to the hotel with her, leaving the Cromptons to digest the tragedy and vent their own emotions.

Remains of the mizzen mast

The Cromptons arranged to have the items that survived shipped to England. They offered to deliver Richard's belong-

*In the cockpit,
the liferaft is
still attached
on the port side.
Main boom is
blocking the
companion
way. The main
hatch is gone.*

ings to his family, if I wanted, whatever I cared to send along. I had taken most of my things off *Hazana* by then, but packing Richard's belongings once again took me on a psychological roller-coaster. I kept trying not to recall when he had worn a certain shirt or shorts. I would catch myself thinking what's the point of packing them up? But, I couldn't just leave everything, for these things would probably mean something to someone in his family.

The F.B.I. was called in because two of us had checked out of Tahiti but only I had checked into Hawaii. As Richard was a British citizen missing in international waters, it was the F.B.I.'s job to investigate. They were very kind as they questioned me intently, but something was wrong. My timeline and theirs for the collision between Hurricane Raymond and *Hazana* and for the events that happened afterwards did not mesh. Through diligent replay and replotting, they finally surmised that I must have been knocked out for twenty-seven hours not the three hours I had always thought. That information shook me up all over again. Twenty-seven hours! No wonder the sea and weather were so much calmer when I came to. Where had my mind been, and where was my lover during that time? There was no way I could have saved Richard. I had been knocked out for more than a day. That meant I was one day off on my navigation, and still—by what, the grace of God, The Voice, myself—I had made it to Hawaii? The Voice was right, here was proof again, that I was meant to live. But why hadn't The Voice told me I was knocked out for twenty-seven hours? Where was The Voice anyway?

A spokesman from *Hokusei Maru*, the Japanese research vessel, that had towed me in, came knocking on *Hazana*'s hull as my mom and I were packing the last of Richard's possessions. The man, handing me a printed invitation for a reception that evening aboard the ship, apologized for the late invitation, but it had taken him a while to trace my steps.

Late that afternoon, Mom, Brian and I arrived at the large commercial quay where the *Hokusei Maru* was docked. As we walked up to the ship we saw a table where guests—the men in dress whites, the women in gowns—were being greeted. We looked down, uncertainly, at our casual clothes as an Asian woman dressed in all her finery asked if she could help me. I handed her the invitation and said, "My name is Tami . . ."

"Oh Tami, Tami!" She excitedly handed us name tags.

"I'm sorry we didn't dress better we . . ."

"No matter. You fine, fine. Please, come in." A man ushered us up the gangplank. On deck a magnificent array of food adorned tables set up along the perimeter of the aft deck, and a stage with a podium and microphone had been set up. Music played, and people were dancing.

As we were escorted to an open bar, we received many inquisitive looks. I heard my name being repeated a couple of times, and then officers and mates from the ship started approaching me. I realized then, that they hadn't recognized me as the ravaged woman they had rescued only a few days ago. Many people came up to see how I was doing and to meet my mother and Brian. I enjoyed a fancy Hawaiian cocktail with an umbrella, and Mom and Brian danced while I shook what seemed like every hand on the ship.

The music suddenly ceased, and the first mate tapping on the microphone drew everyone's attention. He thanked everyone for coming. Speaking in both English and Japanese, he told the audi-

Mom and I, the Captain and the crew of the Hokusei Maru

ence they were celebrating the end of a successful joint research venture involving Japanese and Hawaiian college students. He went on to explain that what made this trip most miraculous was seeing a flare and coming upon a mastless sailboat and sailor, and coming to her, yes—her, aid. The crowd applauded. Many people looked at me with wide smiles. I looked down and peripherally scanned the area—which way could I run?

My mom grabbed my arm. "Smile, honey. It's okay."

The captain walked up to the mike, and the mate translated for us as the captain spoke in animated Japanese. It was the first time in his career, the captain related, that he had seen and helped a shipwrecked sailor. It was an honor to be able to offer the service of his ship and crew, he said, and he would like to present me with a gift. I had no idea I would be honored at this reception. My mom gave me a little shove. I tried to hold my chin up as I walked onto the stage. The captain bowed. I bowed. Then he latched a necklace with a precious pearl pendant around my neck. Tears, the endless tears, flowed to the valley of my neck as I kissed his cheek thank you. Then with much cheer, he proposed a banzai toast, wishing me ten thousand years of good luck.

I waffled among a rainbow of emotions. Here, I was being praised for surviving, but did anyone really understand that some days out there I hadn't wanted to live? Could anyone, besides my mother, see what great grief and guilt I shouldered about Richard's fate? I knew I was going to have to find a way to accept that it was okay that I had lived, but did I deserve ten thousand years of good luck?

I would have liked to say more, to the captain and crew, to expound on how I felt when I saw their ship and the crew's encouraging faces. But all I had the strength to do was finger the pendant and thank them for helping me. The cacophony of the applause was almost as nerve-wracking to me as the hurricane had been, and when the mate approached and offered to take us on a tour of the ship, I eagerly accepted.

I took deep breaths as we climbed up to the pilothouse. Glancing around I was in awe of how high we stood above the sea. I looked down and imagined how tiny and forlorn *Hazana* and I must have looked to the crew and students on the ship.

Tossing and turning that last night in Hilo, I was grateful to see the first hint of dawn. I crawled out of bed and put on the dress Richard had given me the night he proposed in Tahiti. Scrutinizing all the vases of beautiful flowers family and friends had sent me, I focused on one extraordinary bloom: a crimson rose. It wasn't a young, closed bud, but a mature blossom with petals gloriously reaching out to me. A single red rose, the international symbol of love. Its scent woke fond memories, a reminder there is new in the old. I leaned over the gem, its scent swirling in my senses like a warmed brandy on a chilly night. This was the rose for Richard.

I quietly slipped out of the hotel room. As I walked along the road, I felt anxious. If the mist left the air and the palette of the sunrise folded into daylight, the ambiance I needed would be lost. It became a race with the sun. I ran.

Winded, I arrived at the waters' edge. I glanced at the horizon—the sun was surfacing as smoothly as a seal. I watched the swells lap against the breakwater, sending ocean spray over the rocks at its end, launching birds into flight. I inhaled the spicy perfume of the rose once again, and then started walking out on the jetty. I became acutely aware of how much I missed this time of day. More mornings than not, I had been awake on *Hazana*, steering or crying or meditating on the bow. It had been part of my salvation. I missed it. How could I leave this and go home without Richard? How am I going to live without him? My life was a mess. But I had survived. I *did* survive.

Coming to a spot that beckoned me, I crawled down a couple of boulders to a flat rock to sit cross-legged a few feet above the sea. I followed the contours of the granite rocks as they slipped into the lavender water. The sea looked so calm. Richard's soul must love the freedom to wander all over it, all over the world. A glimmer of rouge highlighted a cheek of the sea. Was that Richard smiling at me? Oh, Richard, if only . . . If only my soul had been meant to soar the heaven, earth and sea with you, I'd be there. You know that, don't you? For forty-one days at sea I tried to understand what happened to you, to us. The only thing I could figure out is we fell in love. It's as simple as that. Nothing happened to us but falling in mad, passionate love. I want to say to you I will never, ever, love again, but I am weak. I'm weak, Richard. I don't want to be alone. I don't like being alone. No one to share a sunrise with, a dance with . . . I want to be a mother one day, then a grandmother. I want to watch my garden grow and pet baby puppies and old cats and sing Christmas carols with friends. I want to love life as much as I loved it with you—if that's possible. I have to let go—I have to let you go.

I watched the sun kiss the horizon one last time before it sprung into the air and I sprung to my feet. Pulling off the twine ring Richard had given me, I pressed it to my lips. I swear to God I will always love you, Richard. Choking on my tears I slid the ring up the stem of the exquisite garnet rose. Gently I drew the leaves back through the ring, the circle of love, making sure the stems of the leaves held the ring in place. I inhaled its fragrance one last time and then tossed the rose out into the sea. I watched it drift away from me, bobbing on the textured ocean. The rose and the ring had a mission—to find Richard. The shrill cries of gulls brought me back. I watched them soar and dive before I admitted to myself that I, too, had a mission. It was time to go home.

A Flare at Dawn

Halfway through the midnight watch
I paused to behold the touch of first light upon the horizon.
Clouds obscured the sun's rising.

I sighed, "a good picture is not to be had"
but before my spirits had a chance to sag,

Ahoy, I saw a skyrocket at sea.
Fireworks on the ocean? How could that be?
A bright flare I had spied southeast in the morning sky.

I told my watchmates and raced to my cabin
to fetch my binocs to see what had happened.

Far-off in the dim light of the cloudy dawn
I discerned a sailboat whose masts were gone.

The Hokusei Maru's crew did not speak much English
but we managed to convey that their help was needed.

We hauled the plankton net onto the deck
and steamed toward the boat whose masts were wrecked.

My eyes glowed with wonder as we approached
"Who, through some storm, kept this vessel afloat?"

From where had Hazana set forth?
Perhaps Hilo or some other local port?

At the helm of Hazana was a young woman alone.
Across her bow a heaving line was thrown.

As the vessel came under tow how could we possibly know?

Her fiance was lost at sea.
Across the fierce pacific single-handedly,

From 1200 miles off the Baja coast,
with trades and currents used to the utmost.

A spinnaker pole made fast to the forward hatch
with the top of a sail a little wind did catch.

With fortitude, courage, and seamanship
Tami completed the long, arduous trip.

By Rick Jurik - who saw Tami's flares at dawn.

207

Chapter Twenty-one
Home At Last

It was *Hazana* I never really said good-bye to. *"Hazana"* means deed, exploit or feat in Spanish, and in hindsight she had, uncannily, been named appropriately. If *Hazana* had not been built with such structural integrity she would have sunk and I would have gone down with her. I cannot express in words my respect and love for *Hazana*, and my admiration for Anne Wever and the shipwrights who built *Hazana* in Mr. Wever's shipyard in Holland.

It was a whirlwind exit. The next thing I knew I was on the plane headed for the mainland. I didn't look out the window, down at the sea I had crawled across trying to reach land. I slept, curled up on two seats across from my mom and Brian, keeping my anxiety close to me.

At the San Diego airport, I stepped off the plane to see the tarmac crowded with people, lights and cameras. My dad rushed up, tears on his face, and grabbed me and hugged me, and hugged me, and hugged me. He then guided me to my grandparents, who, as always, knew the right things to say. Many of my family and friends were there to greet me, congratulate me. I can't remember a great deal from this reunion except a feeling of love and support. It was much like The Voice promised me it would be. I spent that night at my grandparents' house in my old bedroom, and then the next day went home to Mom's.

Over the next couple months, as I struggled to rebuild my life, I found I had no life. I was floundering, running around like a madwoman, trying to escape pain and indecision. I stayed home for Thanksgiving and Christmas, all the while feeling an overwhelming compulsion to go to Richard's family and explain to

Arriving at home (This photo courtesy of Charles Starr and The San Diego Union-Tribune)

them face to face what had happened—it was the least I could do. So, in early January I flew to England.

I landed in London and caught a train to Southampton where *Hazana*'s owners, Peter and Christine Crompton lived. From my train window, I watched as England's groomed landscape—so different from the lush wildness of the South Pacific—rushed by.

The Cromptons' home was impressive. The guest room glowed in a warmth of welcome. They were gracious hosts, doing everything to make me comfortable. Peter asked if I'd like to go with them and some friends on a sailboat race around the Isle of Wight. I agreed, and we had a fine time on their racing sloop. We didn't win the race, but we didn't come in last either. None of the Cromptons' friends mentioned *Hazana* or the capsize to me, although I'm sure they all knew about it.

I didn't stay with the Cromptons long as I was anxious to get to Cornwall and Richard's family. The Cromptons could tell I was still suffering; they were compassionate people. And I realized that though *Hazana* had been insured, they too, had suffered a great emotional loss.

From Southampton I took the train to Cornwall. I stayed at Richard's sister Susie's house. It was a tearful reunion. Susie and Richard had been so close—it was hard for her to believe he was dead. She could see I was very unstable—smiling one minute, tearful the next—so we walked and talked, and shared stories. I felt I connected with her.

Richard's father, Mr. Sharp, came over to Susie's shortly after I arrived. As he walked through the dining room door into the living room, I stood up, not knowing what to do—should I hug him or shake his hand? I looked for a resemblance to Richard, but I didn't see one. I started crying and then surprised myself by saying, "How about a hug." He hugged me and patted my back. After a minute, Susie helped ease the situation by having us sit down at the table for lunch. As we ate, the conversation remained light; no one mentioned Richard. All I wanted to do was talk about Richard and have them ask me about him but it was as if a stone wall of denial had been put before me, so I held my tongue.

The next night we met for dinner at the Sharps'. Their home was impressive too. The meal well thought-out and delicious, but I nervously picked at my food. My stomach was in knots in anticipation of what I would say to the gathered family.

After dinner we all sat in the living room, and I finally described the terrible incident blow by blow. I explained how we tried to outrun the hurricane and what a hero Richard had been as he fought so bravely to keep *Hazana* and me from any harm. The family sat and listened. Not a single question was asked. Perhaps their silence was acceptance of the tragedy—I don't know. I was there because in my heart I felt I owed this trip to Richard. He would have wanted me to tell his family firsthand how bravely he died. I know their pain was as deep as mine. I know it could not have been deeper, different yes, but not deeper. I wanted so desperately to connect with them, to find a piece of Richard that was still alive. It was hard to face the fact that an extension of

Richard did not exist.

A couple of nights later I went with the Sharp family to dinner at friends of theirs who had known Richard since he was a boy. The woman took me aside and with tears in her eyes told me how much she had loved him. She said she and her husband had been very proud of Richard for taking off and living his dream. She too could only shake her head in dismay at his sad and untimely death. It meant a great deal to me that she shared her feelings and felt comfortable enough to ask me a couple of questions.

I met with the Sharp's family lawyer and he explained to me that Richard had left *Mayaluga* to Jurrick, Susie's husband, in his will. Later that night I told Jurrick that if he wanted to sell *Mayaluga*, I would buy her because I wanted to continue to sail her around the world, as Richard and I had planned to do. Jurrick told me that we'd work it out.

Richard's father never cried in front of me, nor did Richard's stepmother. This was a very different response from the one I had gotten from my family. It was probably evidence of the British "stiff upper lip." Close to two months had passed since they learned of Richard's death; perhaps I was taking them backwards in their healing process and not forward. I finally realized that I couldn't help them with their healing and they couldn't help me either.

When I returned to San Diego, two weeks later, there was a message for me from Peter and Ann Deeth whom Richard and I had met in Tahiti. I called them back in Antigua, the West Indies, where they owned a hotel. They had seen my interview with Diane Sawyer on the CBS news and they expressed their heartfelt condolences over the loss of Richard. They asked if I planned on going back to Tahiti. I said yes, and that I'd still like to do the brightwork on their boat, *Petrana*, as I had agreed to before Richard and I left Tahiti, if they still wanted it done. They did.

This conversation set me in motion. My parents accepted the fact that I needed to go back to Tahiti, where all my worldly possessions were, but more importantly where our *Mayaluga* was, waiting for me.

Flying into Papeete was extremely emotional for me. As I stared down into the sparkling aqua sea, I could recall every precious moment I had spent with Richard. I grabbed my carry-on bag from the overhead bin, hurried off the plane and out of the airport, and hailed a taxi. I could not get to *Mayaluga* quickly enough. The cab took me to Mataiea. No one was home at Antoinette and Haipade's when I got there, so I walked down to the beach and stood. There floated *Mayaluga*, the beautiful sloop Richard had built from bow to stern. Tears rolled down my face. Tossing my bag in our old dinghy, I dragged it down to the water and rowed like crazy to get to her.

As I opened the companionway hatch, warm air, like a sigh of relief, escaped, brushing past my face. I took a couple of steps down the ladder, sat down and sobbed every last tear out of me. How could Richard not be here? Had I really thought he'd miraculously show up? I felt so totally alone once again.

A couple of hours passed. As I sat in the cockpit I heard the Topa family arrive home. I watched them for a while, and then felt a yearning to go say hello. As I rowed to shore, they all ran out to greet me. It was both a happy and a sad reunion. They had heard about Richard's death. I thanked them for taking such good care of *Mayaluga* and explained I was back now to com-

The Topa family

plete Richard's and my voyage around the world. They did not like the idea of my staying out on the boat alone, at least not while she was moored so near their house. Antoinette convinced me to stay on shore a while and live with their family. She said we needed each other—it was a time of mixed emotions; so I stayed on shore. They set up a mattress on their living room floor and Antoinette brought home a cloth armoire in which to store my clothes. She was right, it was better for me to be around family.

Every morning started like a train: The wheels would slowly begin to chug until the whole household was up to full speed. Crammed into the car were those going to work and those going to school. We'd first head into town and go to Haipade's favorite spot for poisson cru and croissants for breakfast. Then they would drop me off at the boatyard where I was refinishing the brightwork on *Petrana*.

The *Petrana* was a forty-eight-foot Choy Lee ketch. She had many linear feet of teak wood to refinish so I stripped, bleached and sanded with great care and then applied ten coats of varnish. I was so focused on the project that I didn't realize the effect of the blazing tropical sun and I fainted from heat stroke. A man working on another boat saw me collapse and took me to the medical center, where the staff had me drink water and lie down with a cool cloth on my head. The second time

Yacht Petrana, 48' Choy Lee ketch

I started feeling faint, I realized what was happening and quit work for the day. I wasn't as strong as I used to be.

Refinishing *Petrana* was the best thing for me at that time. It kept me functioning and from wallowing in depression when everywhere I turned I was reminded of Richard. When the Deeths arrived they were thrilled at how great *Petrana* looked. They launched her right away, and we spent many nights sitting in the cockpit talking. It felt good to reminisce with people who knew Richard and had shared good times with us.

During this time I wrote letters to Jurrick, Richard's brother-in-law, trying to reach some agreement about purchasing *Mayaluga*. Sadly, Jurrick and I could never agree on a price. He said he couldn't afford to give her away. Funny declaration regarding a gift that was free in the first place. I was adamantly advised, by people who had my well-being at heart, not to pay a fortune for her no matter what sentimental value was involved. It was a very sad, confusing and frustrating time.

Jurrick wrote to tell me he was hiring a man who had previously completed a circumnavigation to fly to Tahiti and sail *Mayaluga* back to England for him. I can't describe how forlorn I felt. I was given a certain amount of time to get my possessions off the boat. I felt kicked off of *Mayaluga*—our *Mayaluga*. I could feel Richard's soul crying.

Boatless and with no direction, the Deeths invited me to meet them in Bora Bora and crew to Fiji with them. I jumped at the offer. I took what was mine off *Mayaluga* and stored it at the Topas, while I decided what to sell and what to ship home. I shipped home my beautiful shell collections, tapas we had purchased in the Marquesas, pictures, letters and items I couldn't part with. With the last of my possessions loaded in the dinghy I went below in *Mayaluga* and knelt at the V-berth. I draped my arm along the cushion and rested my cheek on the bed. This was where I learned about real love. Oh Richard—Richard, Richard, Richard.

With a heavy heart I climbed on a plane and never looked back as I took off for Bora Bora.

The Deeths sailed *Petrana* from Tahiti to Bora Bora with some of their family on board. After their family left and I flew in, we sailed *Petrana* for the atoll of Mopelia, which is also part of the Society Islands group.

Mopelia was magical. We swam in the clear sparkling lagoon, and walked the white sand beaches. I was beginning to heal. We collected eggs from the thousands of tern eggs laying on the coral reefs. The eggs were delicious to eat once you get over the very orange color they turn when they are cooked.

While I spent hours shelling in the sand I contemplated a lot. Mostly my thoughts flowed to Richard and the precious time we shared doing what I was now doing alone. I still felt so empty and confused, but I knew that I was following the right path by getting back to the sea and to the lifestyle I loved.

From Mopelia, we sailed for the atoll Suwarrow to see the home of the famous hermit, the late Tom Neale. When we arrived we found the yacht Fleur d' Ecosse moored in the bay. She belonged to Anne and Ron Falconer, whom Richard and I had met while cruising the Marquesas.

Walking up the beach, we followed crushed coral paths to Neale's hut, where we came upon a large slab of stone. The inscription on the stone read: 1959–1977 Tom Neale lived his dream on this island.

Anne and Ronald had set up house in the two room hut— Anne was about to deliver their first baby. There were chickens running around, and Tom Neale's small garden flourished with vegetables and tropical plants. The Falconers were happy to see me again and to meet the Deeths. Inside the hut they showed us the logbook passing sailors had signed as evidence they had visited the atoll. It was fascinating to see how many sailors had come from far and wide to explore the atoll. Even survivors of yachts gone aground on the reefs had lived in the hut until rescued.

We stayed at Suwarrow for about three days and then sailed for American Samoa, where we could reprovision on our way to

Fiji. The harbor at Pago Pago was dirty and lined with tuna factories, but on an all-day hike over the saddle of the mountain to the other side of the island, we found gorgeous white-sand beaches.

With food lockers bulging, we headed for the Vava'u Islands in the country of Tonga, where we rendezvoused with the Deeths' son, the young skipper of a privately owned hundred-foot yacht, the *Catalina.* The yacht had six crew members and all the toys one could ever wish to play with: Lazers, windsurfers, and fast, Cigarette boats, just to name a few. We enjoyed picnics on the beach, eating gourmet food and playing with all the toys. It was fun to have such decadence in such a remote place.

Fully inundated with sun and fun after ten days of cruising the outer island group of Vava'u, the Deeths and I took off for Suva, Fiji, a seven-hundred-mile sail. The weather was great and the sailing pleasant. I was very comfortable with the Deeths: They were easy, unassuming, and we respected each other's space.

In Suva—a large port, and metropolis, like Papeete—we checked into customs and then walked around the city. In the open air market, where Asian Indians run much of the commerce, our eyes were drawn to the women's brightly colored saris, and our noses twinged at the pungent scent of curry powders and cayenne lining the open aisles.

Sadly the Deeths' vacationing time was coming to an end. When I called my mother and learned that she and Brian were going to get married, I decided to go home. I was pleased she wanted me to be her maid of honor. The Deeths found a safe anchorage and a caretaker for *Petrana.* When they left I stayed on to paint the boat's interior as I had agreed to do. Then I went home to San Diego for the wedding.

On the flight home I wondered if I would ever get used to being in a remote area one minute and flying into suburbia the next. How many miles had I crossed over the past six months? All I ever wanted was to sail forever.

It was wonderful to see my mother in love. She and Brian were married at Brian's parents' house overlooking the Pacific Ocean on Sunset Cliffs, Point Loma, California. I wore a burgundy wraparound silk skirt with hand-painted pictures of bird of paradise flowers on it. The painted flowers flowed around my hips and up onto a matching blouse. My mother wore an ivory lace dress that showed off her shapely figure. She looked beautiful—I was so proud of her.

Brian, now my stepfather, had enrolled in navigation school, in San Diego, to get his hundred-ton captain's license. My mom suggested I enroll too. Why not? I had moved onto my friend's yacht, to give the newlyweds some space, and I wasn't sure what I wanted to do next. I was 24 years old.

I ended up talking to an old friend from the *Sofia* days, Evan, who was skippering a 106-foot three-masted schooner, *Rambler*, on the east coast. The company he worked for, Ocean Research and Education Society (ORES), was looking for licensed mates, and Evan said if I got my hundred-ton license, they would probably hire me. So, I enrolled.

I was the only woman in the class of about fifteen men. I went to school three nights a week, three hours a night, for eight weeks. I found it difficult to study. I couldn't seem to concentrate. So Brian helped by studying with me.

We both passed the captain's exam and three weeks later, I was second mate aboard the research vessel *Rambler*. She was doing scientific work on Silver Bank, an ocean reef about two hundred miles northeast of the Dominican Republic.

I felt relieved to finally have some direction, and I was aboard *Rambler* for three months, from the Dominican Republic to Gloucester, Massachusetts, her home port.

I signed on *Rambler* for another six months as first mate, and we sailed from Gloucester, Massachusetts to Labrador, and back. Sailing around icebergs was very exciting, it helped thaw my frozen heart. After that six months it was time to move on.

Back in San Diego, I spent the next year working with my mother and Brian in their yacht management business and skippering a trimaran charterboat named *Continental 1*. But after all my traveling and exploring I found San Diego too metropolitan. I longed for a slower paced, intimate setting. A location that had more fresh air and nature than concrete.

During that year, I took a trip to San Juan Island, in the northwest corner of the state of Washington, to visit my friend Laura. I was amused she never locked her front door, could take long walks in the forest without fear. She was constantly waving hello to other islanders, who always smiled and waved back. I saw deer, wild turkeys, eagles, otters and whales. My heart sang; it felt like "home." Here was the ocean I could never leave and God's green earth I longed to love.

Back in San Diego the Pacific Northwest lingered in my mind and lulled me to sleep at night. I recalled how the island's dense emerald forest meandered down to the sea. It just seemed to beckon me.

A few months later I moved to San Juan Island, Washington. Now at last, I was really home.

Chapter Twenty-Two

Afterglow

Often I am asked to be a guest speaker at various functions and yacht clubs in the northwest. They want the hurricane survivor to tell her story, *Red Sky in Mourning,* in person. The first thing I stress is that I am not telling my story to scare would-be blue-water sailors. The cruising life is extremely fulfilling, full of adventure, education, freedom and fun. I emphasize that I share my story to inform everyone who goes to sea, man or woman, of the importance of being prepared to assume the captain's role. It is everyone's, including a woman's, responsibility to learn all she can about navigation. She does not need to memorize the theory of navigation as much as the mechanics of using the sextant and interpreting the results. The basics of calculating a line of position, LOP, are a must.

It is also mandatory to know something about how the electronic instruments work and how to interpret them. Knowledge of handling the rigging and sails is too, a must, because like me, you never know what dilemma nature will cast you in.

The question I'm most frequently asked is: "What would you do differently, if you had to do it all over again?"

My first instinct is to say I'd ask Richard to forget the delivery job and go on with our own plans. But that's only with hindsight. So I answer honestly that I would not tease Mother Nature by attempting a long blue-water sail during any portion of the hurricane season. I stress that mother nature is bigger than any of us, and how it's important to cruise within the sailing seasons.

The second question I'm invariably asked is: "If you were in the same situation again at sea (God forbid), what would you do differently? Turn around? Put out a drogue? Have both of you go below? What?"

I have to shake my head at that question because it's a hard question to answer. I have no one answer. I wish Richard would have come below with me, but it's very hard to relinquish control of the helm, especially when you feel the worst is about to be over and the situation is somewhat under control. We flat-out did the best we could. So, I don't know what we could have done differently.

I will never understand why Richard died and I lived, except that he saved my life by having me go below. Richard will always be my hero, and I will always love him, for how can anyone not love forever the person lost in the spring of a relationship? I am grateful to be alive. I believe it was fate—God's will. And after spending forty-one days alone, the only consistent message I had from God, or a higher power, or the universe, or The Voice, is that we, as individuals, *do* have our own destiny. I believe that God does work "in mysterious ways." That is my belief—the tack I sail my life on.

AFTERGLOW

Epilogue

I live a happy and harmonious life in Friday Harbor, San Juan Island, Washington, where I am again in the brightwork business. The process of stripping, sanding and varnishing gives me a sense of accomplishment, and I love working at my own pace, being my own boss and having happy customers.

In 1992 I fell in love with and later married a talented man, Ed Ashcraft. He asked me to dance at the Grange Hall one Friday night. His arm felt strong around my waist, his grip warm and secure. One dance let to another, and another. He builds dream homes for clients and has built one for us. He's a man who treats me like a queen at the most astonishing times and we have similar dreams and goals. We are lovers and friends, and we make each other laugh.

But my greatest achievements, beyond surviving the hurricane, is having given birth to our daughter, Kelli, in 1995 and Brook in 1997.

The last time we took the girls out sailing in our twenty-six-foot quarter-tonner, *Blondie*, Kelli sat on my lap on the starboard side of the cockpit. We were on a beam reach when she eagerly reached out for the teak and spruce tiller. "You want to help me steer, Kelli?" I asked as I guided her tiny hand onto the smooth surface of the arc-shaped wood. Slowly drawing the tiller toward us, I said: "This is up wind." Then pushing the tiller away, I whispered with a sigh: "And this is down wind."

Kelli turned and looked up at me with her daddy's big blue eyes, sensing something different in my voice, perhaps a wistfulness. I looked down into her beautiful, innocent face, wishing I could promise her that her life would always sail on an even keel, but I knew I had to tell her the truth. I kissed her satiny forehead and confessed: "Life is like sailing, love. It's up wind and down wind." She smiled and I smiled, Daddy eased the sheets then went below to get Brook who had just woken from her nap.

Brook was born on a harvest moon at 12:45 P.M., with the amniotic sac still intact.

"It's a rarity," my mid-wife Melinda told us. "Do you know what it means?"

"No," we replied.

"The old wives' tale is that a child born in the caul will never drown or be lost at sea."

My breath caught—Melinda didn't know about my tragedy at sea. I remember reaching for Brook, taking her in my arms and scrutinizing her new born face. She was crinkled up—damp—crying, fair haired like Ed, Kelli and I. I put her to my breast and hugged her securely.

Thank God she will never be lost at sea. For like my mother had said to me, "Tami, if you'd been lost at sea, I would have never, ever, ever, stopped looking for you."

~ Smooth Sailing ~

photo by South Bay Photography

226

Epilogue

Nautical words used in this book

AFT Near the rear or back of the boat.

AMIDSHIPS In the middle of the boat, where she is widest.

ANEMOMETER An instrument that measures wind velocity.

ATOLL A ring-shaped low-lying reef that encloses a lagoon.

BACKSTAY The wire giving aft, or rear, support to the mast.

BACKWINDED Wind flowing from a forward sail onto the lee side, or opposite side to which the wind is blowing, of an after sail.

BAROMETER An instrument that measures atmospheric pressure.

BEAM REACH To sail when the wind is hitting amidship, or the side of the boat.

BEAT To sail in the direction from which the wind is blowing, or as close to the wind as efficiently possible. Often making progress by sailing in a zigzag line.

BILGE The lowest inner part of a boats hull.

BINNACLE A support or pedestal that houses the compass, usually located in the cockpit.

BLOCK A pulley.

BOOM A horizontal pole that extends the foot of a sail.

BOOM CRUTCH A support that holds the boom in place when it's not in use.

BOWSPRIT A spar extending forward from the bow of a ship.

BRIGHTWORK Boat woodwork that is sanded and varnished, not painted.

BULKHEAD A wall separating a boat's cabins that provides athwartships, or side to side, support to the hull.

CLEAT A wooden, metal or plastic fitting to which lines are secured.

CLEVIS PIN A pin secured in a U-shaped fitting to hold an item of rigging.

CLEW The lower corner of a sail, where the sheets, or lines, attach.

COCKPIT The sunken area of a boat's deck where the wheel or tiller are located.

COAMING A low wall around a cockpit, designed to keep out water.

COMPANIONWAY The entry and steps from the deck to the inside of the boat.

CUTTER A sailing boat having one mast, with a mainsail and two headsails, a staysail and a jib.

DEAD RECKONING (D.R.) Calculations of the course sailed, the distance run, the drift of the current and the time spanned to determine a boat's position at sea.

DODGER A windshield, usually of canvas and clear plastic or fiberglass and Plexiglas, used to reduce wind and spray in the cockpit. (Also see windscreen.)

DOLDRUMS No wind.

D-RING Stainless steel D-shaped ring through which a rope may be passed.

DROGUE A drag device, such as a long rope with knots in it, trailed behind a boat to help slow the boat down.

EPIRB Emergency position-indicating radio beacon.

FERRO-CEMENT A mixture of cement, sand, and pozzolan, or fine aggregate, troweled onto a framework of rods, pipes and chicken wire.

FOOT The lower edge of a sail.

FORE In front; opposite of aft.

FORESTAY A stay, usually a stainless steel cable, that runs from the bow, or forward part of a boat, to the top of the mast. (Also see stays.)

GALLEY Kitchen on a boat.

GENOA Genoa jib, also called genny. A large triangular headsail that extends well aft of the mast.

GOOSENECK The universal joint that holds the boom to the mast.

HALYARD A line used to hoist a sail and/or flag.

HAWSER A very thick rope.

HEAD 1) Bathroom. 2) The top corner or edge of a sail.

HEADSAIL A triangular sail set forward of the mainmast.

HEAVE-TO To lash the tiller one way and backwind the headsail the other way, putting you in a stationary position.

HEEL To lean, to list to one side, as in "heeling like a yacht in a gale."

HELM The tiller or steering wheel of a boat.

HYDRAULICS Machinery operated by the movement and force of liquid.

JACK LINE A line or cable that runs the length of the boat; crew members can clip a safety-harness tether to the line for free range of movement on deck.

JIB A triangular sail set on a stay forward of the mast.

KEEL The fore-and-aft member along the center of the bottom of the boat, on which the structure of the boat is built.

KETCH A two-masted boat with the mizzen mast stepped, or placed, forward of the rudderpost. (Also see mizzen mast.)

KNOT A measurement of speed, one nautical mile per hour, about 1.15 statute miles per hour.

LEE The side opposite to that from which the wind blows.

LINE Nautical term for rope.

LIST To lean to one side, as in "the boat was listing badly."

LOGBOOK (LOG) The record book kept of a voyage.

LUFF 1) The side of the sail attached to the mast. 2) The act of pointing the boat into the wind, spilling air out of the sails.

MIZZEN MAST The mast closest to the stern on a ketch or yawl.

MONKEY FIST The knot on the end of a rope, used for throwing.

NAV STATION The area inside the boat designated for navigational purposes.

PITCHPOLE To somersault in the sea, said of a boat.

PORT The left side of a boat.

PULPIT A stainless-steel guardrail around the bow or stern of the boat.

REEF To reduce the size of a sail to lessen the area exposed to the wind.

RODE Rope attached to the anchor chain.

RUDDER An underwater vertically hinged plate of metal or wood that is adjusted by the helm to steer the boat.

RUDDER POST The vertical shaft of a rudder, allowing it to pivot when the tiller or steering gear is operated.

RUN OFF To turn downwind and sail with the wind on your back.

SAT-NAV Satellite navigation. An instrument that receives coordinates from satellites for navigation.

SCHOONER A fore-and-aft-rigged boat having two or more masts, with the mainmast being the tallest or equal to the foremast.

SEAT LOCKER Compartment for stowage located under a seat.

SET Pushed by the current.

SHACKLE A metal U-shaped fitting with an eye in each of its arms through which a pin can be screwed or driven.

SHAKEDOWN CRUISE A test sail.

SHEET A line used to control a sail's position.

SHROUD A wire rope secured from the side of a boat to the masthead, to provide athwartships, or side, support to the mast.

SLOOP A fore-and-aft-rigged boat with one mast and one forward sail or headsail.

SOLE The floor of a boat's cabin.

SPAR Any pole supporting the sail of a boat: for example, a mast, bowsprit or boom.

SPINNAKER A three-cornered sail made of light, stretchy sailcloth, used when running downwind.

SPREADER A wood or metal strut on a mast that keeps the rigging stretched apart.

SQUALL A windstorm, usually brief and violent and often with rain.

STANCHION Metal poles attached to the deck to support the life-lines.

STARBOARD The right side of a boat.

STAY A wire rope that supports a mast forward and aft.

STAYSAIL A triangular sail used between the jib and the mainsail.

TABERNACLE The housing on deck that supports the heel and pivot of a mast so it can be lowered to the deck.

TACK 1) To alter course. 2) The lower-forward corner of a fore-and-aft sail.

TETHER A line attached from a safety vest to the boat.

THRU-HULL A fitting that runs from the interior to the exterior of the hull.

TILLER A lever used to steer a boat.

TOERAIL Raised edge around the deck of a boat.

TRADE WINDS An extremely consistent system of winds occupying most of the tropics.

TRIM To pull in or ease out the sheet of a sail so that the sail will set properly.

V-BERTH Berth in the bow of the boat.

VHF A very high frequency radio, effective, usually, for short distances and within line of sight.

WATERLINE A horizontal line on the hull of a boat, indicating the designed displacement.

WINDLASS A winch that has horizontal drum and can handle chain cable.

WINDSCREEN A dodger that blocks the wind. (Also see° dodger.)

YAWL A two-masted boat with the mizzen mast aft of the rudderpost.

About the Authors

Tami Oldham Ashcraft grew up in San Diego, California. She spent much of her teenage years surfing and spending time on the waterfront. After surfing for a year in Baja California, Mexico, Tami gave up her surfboard for sails. She signed onto a yacht as crew for a thirty-day passage to French Polynesia. During this time her love of sailing developed and has continued to be a priority in her life.

Tami now resides in Friday Harbor, Washington, with her family. In addition to writing, she owns and operates *Brightwork by Tami,* a yacht refinishing business—ideal, as the lure of the sea continues to nourish her.

Susea McGearhart, a free-lance writer and photographer started sailing twenty years ago when she met her husband Gene. After delivering a 43' sloop from San Francisco to Antigua, West Indies, she returned home to Friday Harbor, Washington where she met Tami. Susea's marvelment over Tami's survival encouraged Tami to finally write her heartbreaking story, *Red Sky in Mourning.*

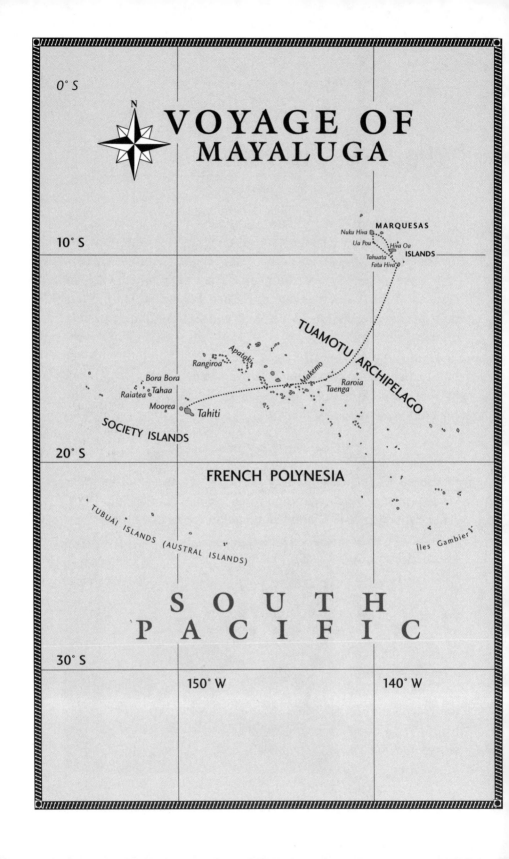

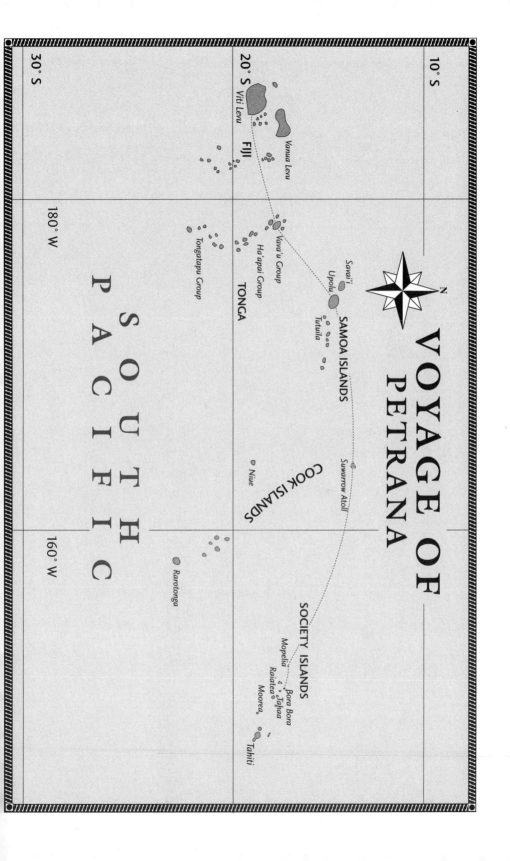

VOYAGE OF PETRANA

N

SOUTH PACIFIC

10° S

20° S

30° S

180° W

160° W

FIJI
Viti Levu
Vanua Levu

TONGA
Vava'u Group
Ha'apai Group
Tongatapu Group

SAMOA ISLANDS
Savai'i
Upolu
Tutuila

COOK ISLANDS
Suwarrow Atoll
Niue
Rarotonga

SOCIETY ISLANDS
Mopelia
Bora Bora
Raiatea
Tahaa
Moorea
Tahiti

BRIGHT WORKS PUBLISHING
Order Form

To order copies of this book, complete this form and FAX it to
360-378-6776
or email us at: ashcraft@rockisland.com with your request

Bright Works Publishing

P.O. Box 2154 Friday Harbor, WA 98250
FAX# (360) 378-6776

Please send me :

Qty	Price **$18.95** each (US)	Amount

TOTAL _____
(WA State Residents add 7.7% Sales Tax)_____
Shipping (see below)_____
TOTAL DUE:$_____

SHIP TO: _____

NAME:_____

ADDRESS:_____

CITY:_____ST:_____ ZIP:_____

DAYTIME PHONE:(   ) _____.
(important)

Shipping Charges:
Priority Mail/First Class: $3.50 for up to two books. Call for larger orders.

Payment:
Check Enclosed in the amount of $_____
Credit Card Orders: Visa or MasterCard Only

Card#_____ ex date:___/___

Signature:_____
Print Your Name:_____

For more information, call **1-360-378-6776**
Email us at: ashcraft@rockisland.com or visit our website at:
www.rockisland.com/~ashcraft